INTRODUCTION

In the United States, legal cannabis sales exploded to an astonishing $17.5 billion in a single year, a meteoric rise of 46% from the year prior. This isn't just a number; it's a beacon, illuminating the seismic shift from taboo to mainstream, from the shadows into the blazing spotlight of legitimate commerce. Why should this matter to you? Because within this green rush lies a labyrinth of opportunity, a chance to carve out your slice of a multi-billion-dollar pie. But where to start in a market so vast, so intricate? Imagine standing at the forefront of this budding industry, a pioneer with soil-stained hands and a vision clearer than the most pristine THC crystal. That's me, Calvin Frye, your guide through the haze, ready to share how I turned a plant into an empire. Are you prepared to plant your flag on this fertile ground, to savor the sweet scent of success? Keep turning the pages, and I'll show you how to cultivate your dreams into towering realities. Just remember, in this industry, the highs are high, the lows... well, let's just say you'll need more than a green thumb to thrive.

In the burgeoning landscape of the cannabis industry, a single plant can be the seed from which a fortune sprouts. As the sun rises over emerald fields, the potential for prosperity is as boundless as the sky above. But what does it truly take to transform this verdant vision into a reality that can weather the storms of regulation, competition, and market volatility?

Consider this: not long ago, the very idea of legal cannabis businesses flourishing across the United States was a pipe dream relegated to the fringes of society. Yet, here we stand, at a crossroads where the once unthinkable has taken root and blossomed into a legitimate, booming industry with projections to soar beyond $30 billion by 2025.

What does this exponential growth mean for you? It signifies a rare confluence of passion and profit, a chance to be part of a green revolution that is not just reshaping laws and attitudes but also creating unprecedented economic opportunities. Whether you're a budding entrepreneur, an investor with a keen eye, or simply curious about this new frontier, the significance of this moment cannot be overstated.

In these pages, I, Calvin Frye, will take you on a journey through the heart of this green giant. With nearly two decades of experience, I've seen the industry's roots entangle with law, society, and commerce, growing into the complex canopy it is today. I will unveil the strategies that have allowed me and others to thrive in this market, the intricacies of licensing, the symbiosis with ancillary businesses, and the personal experiences that have shaped my path.

But what are the real stakes, the hidden traps, and the golden rules in this game of green? How does one navigate the labyrinth of legalities, the nuances of cultivation, and the art of retail in an industry that is still, in many ways, writing its rulebook?

From the fertile soil of California, where the modern cannabis crusade took root, to the bustling streets of Phuket where my dispensary chain now stands, I have woven my narrative through the fabric of this industry. I've been at the negotiating tables, in the labs, and on the front lines of activism. This book is more than a guide; it's a testament to the resilience and ingenuity required to succeed. It's a map to navigate the highs and endure the lows, a chronicle of victories and lessons learned.

As we chart this course together, you will discover how to secure your foothold in this green gold rush. You'll learn about the myriad licenses available, from cultivation to consumption lounges, and how to select the right one for your vision. I'll share insights into the ancillary products and services that are integral yet often overlooked components of the cannabis ecosystem. You'll hear first-hand accounts of the battles fought for legalization and the ongoing struggles for social equity in an industry that is as much about justice as it is about profit.

This is not just a story of personal triumph but a blueprint for the next generation of cannabis entrepreneurs. It's a look into the future of an industry still in its youth, growing faster than the plants at its core.

So, take a deep breath. The journey to make millions in the cannabis industry starts now, with one simple step: Turn the page. Let's begin.

CONTENTS

Copyrights   VI

Title Page   VII

Preface   VIII

1. Bum-Rushing the Show : Entering the Cannabis Market   1

2. Cultivating Success: Exploring the Main License Types   13

3. Making That Dough: Financial Strategies   34

4. Biggest Key to Success: Marketing and Branding   47

5. Involving the Hemp Industry: CBD and THC Cross Over Products   67

6. The People's Plant: Social Equity and Advocacy   79

7. The Global Green Opportunity: International Markets and Expansion   91

8. Insider Tips on Making Millions in the Cannabis Industry   103

About the Author   115

Acknowledgements   117

Endnotes   118

How to Make Millions in the Cannabis Industry

As told from one of the first Cannabis Businesses in the US

Calvin Frye

IngramSpark

Ingram Spark

PREFACE

I am excited about writing this book on the introduction to the cannabis industry after attending so many trade shows and conferences throughout the years. I finally began to Keynote and moderate some of the biggest trade shows in the United States. One thing I learned from doing so many trade shows and talking to so many people after my keynotes or seminars was that there is a serious need for accurate information for people looking to get into this industry. I am one of the pioneers of the cannabis industry in the United States. I had one of the first cannabis businesses in the country back in 2005. Long before there was a Colorado, Washington, Oregon, or any of the initial states that eventually gave out actual cannabis licenses, there were the pioneers that started the industry in California. Ever since the Compassionate Use Act of 1996 was enacted in California we have been trying to figure out a way to get the ball rolling, so that people would have safe access to cannabis as a medicine. Over the years as the taboo was erased, and the stigma began to fade on marijuana in general, states began to see the profitability in the cannabis market and began to put cannabis on the ballot and let the people make the choice. Luckily for all of us, the people voted in favor of cannabis legalization, and now cannabis is one of the hottest businesses in the world. I have starred in documentaries (Super High Me), and reality TV shows as well as made many public appearances across the country. I have run a successful cannabis business, and now a micro business as California began to hand out real licenses.

I have seen it all, I have sat in meetings with multi-million dollar corporations and talked to billion-dollar CEOs within the industry to find out what it truly takes to make a successful cannabis business. Now I finally put together a book that acts as a guide to choosing the right cannabis license, possibly choosing even an ancillary business within the space, or simply teaming up with a license holder and starting your own brand. I will discuss the correct steps to take to start a cannabis business, as well as share some of my personal stories, that I have gone through to make me what I am today, a successful cannabis pioneer and a well-respected operator within the national and global cannabis community.

CHAPTER ONE

BUM-RUSHING THE SHOW : ENTERING THE CANNABIS MARKET

The Reality of the Cannabis Industry

B eing one of the first cannabis businesses in the United States, traveling the country, helping write regulations, and speaking on the subject, has given me great insight into the reality of the cannabis business. One of the biggest concerns that I see with every single person who approaches me after a keynote, seminar, or speaking session is that they don't understand what this industry entails. There are so many books, pamphlets, and conventions these days with people who gather their experiences from reading books or talking to friends who are in the business or who want to be in the business that the answers they get from these people are often varied and incorrect. Because of the federal illegality of this industry, hard-core standard guidelines vary from state to state so a lot of people get confused as to what the actual truth is when it comes to rules and regulations within the industry, so what I wanted to do was to put together some information from a person who has been in the industry from day one. Combine that with all of the seminars and meetings with governors, senators, and rule makers from various states throughout the United States, as well as internationally to try to put this into a single concise book so that people can stop wasting time and wasting fortunes on trying to get rich quick with limited and inaccurate information.

Understanding the Legal Landscape Federal Laws

At the federal level, cannabis is classified as a Schedule I drug under the Controlled Substances Act, which means it is considered to have a high potential for abuse and no accepted medical use. This classification creates legal complications for cannabis-related businesses, including issues related to financing, production, transport, and sale of cannabis products. Despite this, the federal government has largely allowed states to enact their cannabis laws without interference. The Agricultural Improvement Act of 2018, also known as the 2018 Farm Bill, federally legalized hemp, a subtype of cannabis, as a legal agricultural commodity. The Food and Drug Administration (FDA) regulates cannabis and cannabis-derived products, including cannabidiol (CBD)

State Laws

State laws regarding cannabis vary widely, with nearly all states having passed some level of legalization, ranging from medical and/or recreational use to permitting the use of low-THC products. Some states have also implemented regulations such as potency caps, time-based sales limits, taxes based on potency, and seed-to-sale tracking systems

Licensing and Business Requirements

Cannabis businesses are subject to various licensing, permit, and registration requirements, which can vary by state and even by city or county. These requirements are put in place for public safety, tax, and other reasons. Compliance with these requirements is essential for operating legally

Conflict of Laws

The conflict between federal and state laws creates a complex legal landscape for cannabis businesses. For example, while a state may have legalized cannabis, cannabis-related businesses in that state may still face potential legal complications due to the federal classification of cannabis as a Schedule I drug. In conclusion, the legal landscape of the cannabis industry is complex and constantly evolving. Businesses in this industry need to stay informed about changes in laws and regulations at all levels of government. The legal landscape of the cannabis industry is complex and constantly evolving. Currently, cannabis is classified as a Schedule I drug at the federal level, which creates legal complications for businesses in the industry. However, the federal government has largely allowed states to enact their cannabis laws without interference. Additionally, the 2018 Farm Bill federally legalized hemp, a subtype of cannabis, as a legal agricultural commodity. State laws regarding cannabis vary widely, with many states having passed some level of legalization. Cannabis businesses must navigate the complex and ever-changing legal landscape of cannabis. It is anticipated that shortly, there will be a push for more comprehensive federal legalization of cannabis, which would alleviate some of the conflicts between federal and state laws.

This would provide a clearer regulatory framework for cannabis businesses and open up new opportunities for growth and expansion in the industry. However, this transition will likely be gradual and will require careful consideration of various factors, including public health, social equity, and economic impacts... Only time will tell. I am encouraged by the rhetoric from President Biden a couple of months ago on the possibility of finally rescheduling cannabis...fingers crossed!

Choosing Your Cannabis Business Model

There are two main categories of cannabis businesses: those that touch the plant (like cultivation, manufacturing, and dispensaries) and those that do not (like packaging, construction, and professional services) For example, a cultivation business breeds, grows, and harvests cannabis, while a dispensary sells cannabis products to consumers. Ancillary businesses, on the other hand, might provide packaging for cannabis products or build out cultivation facilities. In the ever-evolving landscape of the cannabis industry, it is projected that ancillary businesses will play a significant role in the coming years. As the demand for cannabis products continues to rise, so will the need for innovative packaging solutions and state-of-the-art cultivation facilities. With legalization spreading across regions and countries, ancillary businesses will capitalize on this lucrative market by offering specialized services and expertise to support the growing cannabis industry. As entrepreneurs and investors recognize the untapped potential of these auxiliary ventures, they will actively seek opportunities within the ancillary sector. This will lead to a surge in startups and investments in areas such as cannabis packaging, construction, consulting, and technology. These ancillary businesses will not only provide essential support services but also contribute to the overall growth and professionalism of the

cannabis industry. As regulations become more standardized and the stigma surrounding cannabis continues to diminish, ancillary businesses will emerge as key players in this ever-expanding market. They will bring innovation, efficiency, and expertise to the industry, ultimately fueling the continued growth and normalization of the cannabis industry worldwide.

Licensing and Compliance: Your Pathway to Legitimacy

Times have changed since some of the very first cannabis businesses opened here in the United States. In California back when this industry first started, there was no application process. All we had was the Compassionate Use Act of 1996, in which the people of California voted to allow medical marijuana usage for patients whom it helped. We started with co-ops and collectives of people growing marijuana for each other as needed. A few brave soldiers like myself and other people like Don Duncan, DeAngelo from Harborside, and Pioneers like Dennis Peron were the first people to call ourselves having what is now called a legal Dispensary. At that time there were no applications or licenses at all so you just had to apply for some type of regular business license so that you could operate as a legal business entity within whichever local jurisdiction you were in. Those times are long gone, and after real legalization happened and rules and regulations were put in by states, just opening a dispensary was no longer legal. Now there is an application process that an individual or group of individuals have to adhere to. Now an application must be turned in and it is usually pretty extensive. In today's market, most people have to hire an application writing person or legal firm to help them prepare their application to be considered by the state. Because there is so much competition in most states, now they have a legal limit as to how many licenses they are going to admit. Now the application process is crucial. I remember talking to one of the very first and most successful application writing companies at the time, SIVA, based out of Glendale, California. The owner, whose name was Avis, who is still a good friend of mine, whom I occasionally talk to was known for his high success rate and getting licenses for people that wanted them in different states. During those times, the license writing fee was quite substantial. One of the first things that a person needs to consider if they are going to go for a license in a state in which there is a limit on licenses is to make sure that they are financially able to go for a license because a lot of the states don't refund your fee if you don't get a license. That could be a very big hit to someone if they spend a lot of money trying to get a license and don't receive it. Here are some of the things you need to consider when you're applying for a cannabis license via a cannabis license application.

1. Understanding Local and State Regulations: It's crucial to understand the specific regulations and requirements of the state and local jurisdiction where you plan to operate your cannabis business. These regulations vary widely, and non-compliance can lead to application rejection or legal issues.

2. Business Formation: Depending on the jurisdiction, you may need to establish your business entity before applying for a license. This

includes registering your business with the appropriate state agencies and obtaining federal and state taxpayer identification numbers.

3. License Type: The type of license you need depends on the nature of your cannabis business. This could range from cultivation, manufacturing, distribution, and retail, to ancillary products. Some jurisdictions may limit the number of certain types of licenses.

4. Application Details: Your application should include detailed information about your business, including your operating procedures, business model, and financial projections.

You may also need to provide proof of a legal right to use the proposed location and proof of bond.

1. Background Checks: Most jurisdictions require background checks for all business owners and key employees. This ensures that those involved in the business have not been involved in illegal activities that could pose a risk to the business or the public.

2. Local Approval: In some areas, you may need to obtain local approval before you can apply for a state license. This could involve obtaining a local permit or meeting specific zoning requirements.

3. Financial Projections and Funding: You should be prepared to provide detailed financial projections as part of your application. Additionally, securing funding for your cannabis business can be challenging due to federal regulations, so you'll need to explore alternative funding options.

4. Team Structure: Your application should include information about your team structure, including the roles and responsibilities of each team member.

5. Regulatory Compliance: Your application should demonstrate your

understanding of and compliance with all relevant cannabis regulations. This includes your plans for tracking and reporting, security, waste disposal, and more.

6. Social Equity Programs: Some jurisdictions offer benefits for applicants who qualify for social equity programs. These programs aim to address the impacts of the prohibition of cannabis on certain communities.

Applying for licenses and permits involves meeting the specific requirements set by your state and local government. For example, a cultivation business might need a license based on the type of production and lighting used, the number of plants grown, or the size of the canopy. A dispensary, on the other hand, might need a storefront retailer license.

Licensing Requirements

Most cannabis businesses are subject to various licensing, permit, and registration requirements, which are put in place for public safety, tax, or other reasons. These requirements can vary by state and even by city or county. For example, in California, the Department of Cannabis Control is responsible for licensing businesses that are cultivating medicinal and adult-use cannabis. Licensing can differ based on the category of the business, whether you're cultivating, selling, manufacturing, or investing. Therefore, it's crucial to understand the specific licensing requirements for your type of business in your specific location.

Compliance

Compliance refers to adhering to state and local regulations, laws, and requirements regarding the cultivation, production, and sale of cannabis products. This includes regulations related to inventory tracking, transportation, security, waste destruction, quality control, employment, training, recordkeeping, and emergency response. Non- Non-compliance can result in serious consequences, including hefty fines, loss of license, and even criminal charges. It can also damage a retailer's reputation. Therefore, it's essential to create lasting programs that guide a cannabis business's current and future operations.

Ensuring Compliance

To ensure compliance, businesses can conduct regular self-audits, maintain thorough documentation, and stay informed about changes in regulations. It's also recommended to seek professional guidance, as the cannabis industry is evolving quickly and regulations can change frequently. Banks that do business with legalized cannabis dispensaries should perform due diligence on marijuana businesses, reviewing the business' licensing materials and registration procedures for potential red flags. In conclusion, obtaining a license and ensuring compliance are critical steps for establishing and maintaining legitimacy in the cannabis industry. It's important to stay informed about changes in laws and regulations, conduct regular self-audits, and seek professional guidance as needed. to maintain trust and credibility. Professional guidance and self-audits will become standard practices, helping businesses mitigate risks and ensure their long-term adherence to the cannabis In the future, as the cannabis industry continues to evolve, licensing and compliance requirements for businesses in this sector are expected to become even more stringent. States and local governments will likely impose stricter regulations, and businesses will need to demonstrate their commitment to compliance to maintain legitimacy and gain trust in the marketplace.

On a more personal note, when it comes to compliance one of the biggest mistakes that I ever made was teaming up with another group that I hired to manage my place. This management team that I partnered with promised the world and showed me resumes and people that they claimed were top-notch in making sure that the facility would be in full compliance. Unfortunately, as time went on some of the workers that had known me for a long time before I brought the other group on board. They were beginning to feel uneasy about some of the things they saw going on in my location. Fortunately, for me, I had access to security cameras and could watch them at any time as well as so I rewinded the tape to see what was going on. My new partners had forgotten that I had access to the DVR system, and lo and behold they were doing things that were sketchy and borderline illegal. After confronting them, our relationship took a turn for the worst, and luckily, I was able to gather enough information to take them to court and remove them from my premises. At that time I had been in business for well over a decade and I could've lost everything by operating outside of compliance. So my lesson to anyone that's going to start your business, make sure that you do your due diligence on anyone that you're going to hire as a management team and keep your eyes on things from afar just to make sure things are operating on the up and up.

Building Your Cannabusiness Team

Building a team involves hiring individuals with the skills and expertise needed to operate your cannabis business. This might include cultivators for a cultivation business, budtenders for a dispensary, or professionals with experience in cannabis law and regulations. As with any business, having a good team and access to what you need is crucial, the cannabis industry is a multi-billion dollar industry just like the NFL, the tech industry, and any other high-money value industry. That means you have to have the correct team surrounding you to succeed. You can have the best CEO in the world but if you're on board and your employees are subpar your business will still not flow. You could have the best quarterback and running back in the NFL but if you're offensive line is not blocking for you, you still won't reach your potential. These analogies are the same for the cannabis industry. I am going on year 19 in this industry And I have had many employees throughout that time. You must understand the cannabis business and understand that this is also a retail business so customer service and reliability are premium. Now that this is a highly regulated and compliant industry the people that you have on those teams are paramount to whether your business is successful or not. You need a very good management team that understands how a business runs in general from inventory control to managing personnel to training. You need budtenders and product handlers who actually are very familiar with the product and can actively converse with the patients or customers who need information on what you are selling. If you're cultivating, then you need a team of individuals who are familiar with growing and the little minute things that can produce a quality product. In the manufacturing realm, you need someone who understands GMP practices so that you can create a quality product. You need someone who understands how to advertise and market because of the competition in the regular market as well as the black market to convince someone to shop at your facility. Having a good company team is crucial in the cannabis business for several reasons:

1. Navigating a Rapidly Changing Industry: The cannabis industry is rapidly evolving, with new regulations, technologies, and market trends emerging regularly. A strong team can help a business navigate these changes effectively and stay ahead of the competition.

2. Attracting and Retaining Talent: A positive company culture can help attract top talent and reduce staff turnover, which can be costly and disruptive. Employees are more likely to stay with a company if they feel valued, supported, and connected to the company's mission.

3. Enhancing Productivity and Creativity: When employees are engaged and feel a sense of belonging, they are more likely to invest their time and energy in their work. This can lead to increased productivity, creativity, and a shared commitment to achieving common goals.

4. Promoting Collaboration: A good team promotes collaboration, which can lead to better decision-making and problem-solving. Cross-training employees in different areas of the business can also enhance communication and understanding across departments.

5. Ensuring Compliance: The cannabis industry is heavily regulated, and non-compliance can lead to serious legal and financial consequences. A knowledgeable and experienced team can help ensure that a business stays compliant with all relevant laws and regulations.

6. Leadership: Effective leadership is crucial in the cannabis industry. Leaders need to be able to guide their teams through the unique challenges of the industry, from regulatory hurdles to scaling operations. They also need to demonstrate empathy and understanding, as turnover is notoriously high in the cannabis industry.

7. Financial Management: A good team can also help with financial management, which is particularly important given the challenges of securing funding in the cannabis industry. This can include everything from financial planning and analysis to securing investments. In the rapidly evolving cannabis industry, building a strong team is crucial for success. A team can help navigate the changing regulations, attract and retain top talent, enhance productivity and creativity, promote collaboration, ensure compliance with laws, provide effective leadership, and

manage finances effectively. With the right team in place, a cannabis business can thrive in this multi-billion dollar industry. As the industry continues to grow and mature, the demand for skilled professionals will only increase, making it even more important to invest in building and developing a strong team.

Chapter Two

CULTIVATING SUCCESS: EXPLORING THE MAIN LICENSE TYPES

Mastering Cannabis Cultivation

C ultivation and genetics are very important to the cannabis process. If your genetics suck then your final product will suffer regardless of how high-tech your facility is. Cannabis cultivation is the process of growing cannabis plants, which can be used for a variety of purposes, including medical and recreational use. The cultivation process involves several steps and requires careful attention to environmental conditions, plant health, and regulatory compliance. Preparing the Soil and Growing Medium: The first step in cannabis cultivation is preparing the soil or growing medium. This involves ensuring the soil has the right nutrients and pH balance for cannabis plants to thrive.

Planting Seeds or Clones: Cannabis plants can be grown from seeds or clones (cuttings from a mature plant). The choice between seeds and clones depends on various factors, including the desired strain, available resources, and cultivation experience.

Irrigating, Fertilizing, and Managing Pests: Cannabis plants require regular watering and fertilization to grow. Pest management is also crucial to prevent damage to the plants and ensure a healthy crop.

Harvesting Plants: Once the plants have matured, they are harvested. The timing of the harvest is important to ensure the highest potency and yield.

Drying, Curing, and Trimming Plants: After harvest, the cannabis plants are dried and cured to develop their flavors and aromas. The plants are also trimmed to remove excess leaves and prepare the buds for sale. Cannabis cultivation involves various techniques, each with its unique benefits and challenges. Here are some of the most common methods:

Soil Cultivation: This is the traditional method of growing cannabis, where the plant is grown in soil, either indoors or outdoors. The soil is usually specially prepared with a mix of nutrients to boost growth and yield. However, soil cultivation may not offer as much control over the plant's growth conditions, and there's a risk of overwatering.

Hydroponics: In hydroponic cultivation, cannabis plants are grown without soil. Instead, the plants are suspended using a growing medium like rock wool or coco coir, which helps anchor the plant and deliver nutrients and oxygen to the roots. This method offers more control over the plant's growth conditions but requires more maintenance and expertise.

Aeroponics: This advanced cultivation method involves suspending the plants in the air and spraying water and fertilizer over the roots. It's known for producing high yields, but it's also the most complex and expensive method.

Aquaponics: Aquaponics combines the cultivation of plants with fish breeding. In this method, cannabis plants are grown in an aquatic environment without inert support. The nutrients come directly from the water, in connection with the positive effects of the presence and activity of fish. While this method can be expensive and complex, it can also be rewarding for home growers.

Screen of Green (SCROG): This training and trellising technique involves growing many small plants instead of a few larger ones. The plants are trained during the vegetative stage to form a green "screen," which helps to maximize light exposure and increase yield.

Sea of Green (SOG): Similar to SCROG, the SOG method involves growing many small plants to maximize space efficiency. However, unlike SCROG, the plants are not trained and are allowed to grow naturally.

Super Cropping: This high-stress training technique involves damaging the plant in a controlled way to encourage it to grow more branches, increase its yield, and become more resistant to disease.

Low-Stress Training (LST): LST involves bending and tying the plants to control their shape and expose more of the plant to light, which can increase yield without stressing the plant as much as other methods.

Each of these methods has its advantages and disadvantages, and the best method for a particular grower will depend on their resources, expertise, and the specific requirements of the cannabis strain they are growing. Most major cultivation grows use hydroponics so here are some of the advantages and disadvantages below:

Hydroponic cannabis cultivation is a method of growing cannabis plants without soil, using nutrient-rich water solutions. This technique has several advantages and disadvantages:

Advantages of Hydroponic Cannabis Cultivation

1. Control Over Nutrients: Hydroponic systems allow growers to precisely control the nutrients

2. their plants receive, optimizing fertilization and correcting any excesses

or deficiencies.

3. Faster Growth: Plants in hydroponic systems often grow faster due to more efficient nutrient uptake compared to soil-grown plants.

4. Increased Yields: Hydroponic systems can lead to larger yields as plants can absorb nutrients more effectively and are not limited by soil quality.

5. Space Efficiency: Hydroponic systems can be more space-efficient, allowing for more plants per area since roots require less room compared to soil-based systems.

6. Reduced Pest Problems: With no soil, there's a lower risk of soil-borne pests, potentially reducing the need for pesticides.

7. Cleaner Growing Environment: Hydroponics is a cleaner method of cultivation without the mess associated with soil.

8. More Oxygen to Roots: The roots in a hydroponic system receive more oxygen, which can benefit plant growth.

9. Potential for Higher Potency: Some growers believe that hydroponic cultivation can lead to higher potency due to the plant's increased access to nutrients and optimal growing conditions.

Disadvantages of Hydroponic Cannabis Cultivation

1. High Initial Setup Costs: The initial investment for a hydroponic system can be significant, as it requires specialized equipment such as water pumps, lighting systems, and nutrient delivery systems.

2. Complexity and Learning Curve: Hydroponic systems can be complex and may have a steep learning curve for new growers. It requires a good understanding of the science behind plant nutrition and growth.

3. Risk of Equipment Failure: Hydroponic systems rely heavily on equipment, which can fail and potentially harm the plants if not quickly addressed.

4. Temperature Sensitivity: The roots in hydroponic systems grow better within a specific temperature range, and deviations can affect plant health.

5. Costly Mistakes: Errors in a hydroponic system, such as over-fertiliza-

tion or incorrect pH levels, can be more damaging compared to soil, where there's a natural buffering capacity.

6. Waterborne Diseases: While soil-borne pests are less of an issue, hydroponic systems can be susceptible to waterborne diseases, which can spread quickly if not managed properly.

7. Energy Consumption: Hydroponic systems may require more energy for pumps, lighting, and climate control, which can increase operating costs.

In summary, hydroponic cannabis cultivation offers growers more control over the growing environment and can lead to faster growth and higher yields. However, it also comes with higher initial costs, complexity, and potential risks that require careful management.

Cannabis cultivation can be done indoors or outdoors. Indoor cultivation allows for greater control over environmental conditions, such as light, temperature, and humidity, and is often used in regulated markets. Outdoor cultivation, on the other hand, can be more cost-effective and environmentally friendly, but it is subject to weather conditions and seasonal changes. Cannabis cultivation can also lead to environmental concerns due to the release of biogenic volatile organic compounds (BVOCs). These compounds can contribute to the formation of ground-level ozone, particulate matter, and objectionable odors. In addition to the cultivation process, cannabis cultivators must also navigate a

complex regulatory landscape. This includes obtaining the necessary licenses and permits, complying with land use and environmental regulations, and managing the financial and operational aspects of running a cultivation business. Overall, cannabis cultivation is a complex process that requires a deep understanding of plant biology, cultivation techniques, and industry regulations. It also requires a significant investment in time, resources, and expertise.

A little side story when it comes to cultivation... Back in 2005 before the cannabis industry started in the United States, genetics and cultivation were always a big thing in California. Most of the magazines that you would love to read in your basement or in some private setting like High Times magazine, etc., all the pictures of genetics were pretty fascinating. When I opened in 2005 the cannabis laws were untested. Because California was always the hub of cannabis and still is to this day, genetics was a big issue. Towards the end of 2006 in California, because of the dispensary boom I knew I needed to have an edge on my competitors. I used to get so many calls from patients throughout California who wanted to grow their cannabis because of the laws in California at that time I had to start selling genetics in my dispensary. I created a department within my dispensary called Cloneville. Ironically, during that time, there was a popular app on mobile devices called FarmVille. One day I got a call from my copyright attorney telling me that The owners of FarmVille wanted to sue me because they thought I was copying their app.

When my lawyer informed the Federal Copyright Trademark Bureau that this was indeed a cannabis business eventually the Farmville guys dropped their lawsuit. Just another crazy story within the cannabis industry during the early days. Now that cannabis is widespread nationally as well as worldwide, having your genetics is a big deal and one of the reasons that a person may want to consider the cultivation end of the business. The reason is that if you can get into genetics and create very popular strains you can increase your revenue streams by being able to offer branded clones to other businesses.

Manufacturing

Cannabis manufacturing refers to the process of transforming raw cannabis plants into a variety of products. This process involves several stages, including extraction, infusion, packaging, and labeling

Extraction

Extraction is the process of separating cannabinoids and terpenes from the cannabis plant to create a concentrated extract. This can be done using various methods, such as solvent-based extraction (using substances like carbon dioxide, ethanol, or butane), or non-solvent methods like ice water extraction

Infusion

Infusion involves incorporating the cannabis extract into other substances to create a variety of products. This could include infusing the extract into food and beverages, lotions and balms, or other mediums

Packaging and Labeling

Once the cannabis products are created, they need to be packaged and labeled. Packaging must be child-resistant, tamper-evident, resealable (if it contains multiple servings), and opaque (if it is an edible) Labeling is crucial to inform consumers about what they're buying or using. Labels typically include information about the product's cannabinoid content, ingredients, and usage instructions

Types of Products

1. Flower: This is the most traditional form of cannabis, which is the dried and cured buds of the cannabis plant. It's typically smoked or vaporized

2. Edibles: These are food and beverages infused with cannabis. They can come in many forms, including baked goods, candies, chocolates, gummies, mints, and drink additives

3. Concentrates: These are highly potent forms of cannabis made by extracting cannabinoids and terpenes from the cannabis plant. Examples include vape cartridges, dab, shatter, and wax

4. Tinctures: These are alcohol-based cannabis extracts that are typically applied under the tongue for quick absorption

5. Topicals: These are cannabis-infused products designed for application on the skin. They include lotions, creams, balms, and patchesPills and Tablets: These are ingestible forms of cannabis that are often used for medical purposes. They provide a controlled dosage of cannabinoids.

6. CBD Products: These are products made from the non-psychoactive cannabinoid CBD. They can come in various forms, including oils, gummies, and topicals. CBD products can be full-spectrum (containing all parts of the cannabis plant, including up to 0.3% THC), broad-spectrum (containing most of the cannabis plant compounds but with trace amounts of THC), or isolates (containing only CBD)

7. Industrial Hemp Products: These are products made from cannabis plants selected to produce an abundance of fiber. They are used in a variety of applications, from textiles to building materials

Regulatory Considerations

Cannabis manufacturing is heavily regulated, and manufacturers must comply with a variety of laws and regulations. In the United States, for example, manufacturers need a specific license to make cannabis products, and the type of license required depends on the activities they perform and the types of chemicals they use

Challenges and Considerations

Cannabis manufacturing can be complex and requires a good understanding of the science behind plant nutrition and growth. It also involves significant initial investment in specialized equipment, such as extraction machines and packaging systems Furthermore, the cannabis manufacturing industry faces an uncertain regulatory environment and price fluctuations. In conclusion, cannabis manufacturing is a multifaceted process that involves extracting valuable compounds from the cannabis plant, infusing these compounds into various products, and packaging and labeling these products for consumer use. It requires significant expertise, investment, and regulatory compliance. The integration of technology and automation will streamline the manufacturing process, making it more efficient and cost-effective. Additionally, as research and understanding of cannabis compounds continue to expand, we can

anticipate the development of new and innovative products that cater to specific consumer needs and preferences. With the industry poised for continued growth and acceptance, the future of cannabis manufacturing is undoubtedly bright and full of possibilities. Moving forward, the future of cannabis manufacturing holds a plethora of possibilities. As technology and automation continue to advance, the manufacturing process will become more streamlined, efficient, and cost-effective. With the expanding research and understanding of cannabis compounds, we can expect the development of new and innovative products that cater to specific consumer needs and preferences.

Furthermore, as the industry gains more acceptance and undergoes regulatory changes, the growth of the cannabis manufacturing sector is inevitable. The integration of sustainability practices and eco-friendly packaging solutions will revolutionize the industry, leading to a more environmentally conscious approach to cannabis manufacturing. The future of cannabis manufacturing is bright with endless possibilities of product innovation, improved efficiency, and sustainable practices.

Retail Dispensary

Back in the early pioneering days of the cannabis industry in California, a dispensary as it is called now, where the first quasi-legal business. After the ' Compassionate Use Act of 1996" was passed thanks to all of the hard work of my friend and cannabis pioneer Dennis Peron, a few of us in Oakland, Berkley, West Hollywood, and Los Angeles were brave enough to open the very first places to sell cannabis. Senate Bill 420, pun intended, allowed for co-ops and collectives to be established, which then led to the name "Dispensary" to be used in later legislation. I remember when that name was agreed upon by pioneers like Don Duncan, who headed the LA leg of Americans for Safe Access, and Dege" another hardcore activist in a church in Silverlake, CA...aww the good ol days!

A retail cannabis dispensary is a licensed business where customers can legally purchase cannabis and cannabis-infused products. These dispensaries can sell a variety of products, including dried flower, edibles, concentrates, tinctures, topicals, and more.

Opening a retail cannabis dispensary involves several steps:

Obtaining a License: The first step is to obtain a cannabis dispensary license from the relevant state authority. The licensing process varies by state and may involve a competitive application process

Creating a Business Plan: A comprehensive business plan is crucial. It should include details about the market need and opportunity, brand identity, target market, location, execution strategy, and financial projections.

Securing Financing: Opening a dispensary can be expensive, and securing sufficient financing is a critical step. This could involve personal savings, loans, or investments.

Finding a Suitable Location: The location of the dispensary must comply with state and local regulations, which often stipulate how close a dispensary can be to schools, parks, or other public facilities

Complying with Regulations: Dispensaries must comply with a range of regulations, including security requirements, product tracking, and reporting. They must also ensure that all cannabis products are tested for safety and potency.

Hiring Staff: Dispensaries need knowledgeable and professional staff to operate. In some states, staff may need to undergo specific training or certification

Stocking Inventory: Dispensaries must source their products from licensed cannabis growers and manufacturers. Inventory management is crucial to ensure a consistent supply of products to meet customer demand

Opening for Business: Once all the above steps are completed, the dispensary can open for business. Ongoing operations will involve marketing, customer service, compliance with regulatory changes, and regular financial management.

It's important to note that the specifics of opening a retail cannabis dispensary can vary significantly depending on the state, as each state has its cannabis laws and regulations. Therefore, potential dispensary owners should thoroughly research the specific requirements in their state before proceeding.

Looking ahead, the retail cannabis industry is expected to experience continued growth and expansion. As more states legalize cannabis for both medical and recreational use, the demand for retail cannabis dispensaries is likely to increase. The market will become more competitive, leading to innovations in product offerings and customer experience. Additionally, there may be changes in regulations and licensing processes as the industry matures. As the cannabis market evolves, it will be crucial for dispensary owners to stay informed, adapt to changing regulations, and provide high-quality products.

The above-mentioned licenses can be sought after separately but there is a such license as a Microbusiness license that is a combination of licenses. Though I started as a dispensary, I switched over to a microbusiness as soon as the laws changed. This allowed me to be vertically integrated so that I could be a self-supported business as well as cut down on cost. Below are some of the advantages and disadvantages of a Microbusiness:

A cannabis microbusiness is a smaller-scale operation that typically engages in multiple aspects of the cannabis industry, such as cultivation, processing, and retail, all under one license. This model is often referred to as vertical integration

Advantages of a Cannabis Microbusiness

1. Control Over Production: Microbusinesses have control over the entire production process, from cultivation to sale, which can lead to better quality control and product consistency.

2. Local Craft Focus: Microbusinesses can focus on producing artisanal, craft cannabis products, which can appeal to consumers seeking high-quality, locally produced goods.

3. Lower Barriers to Entry: Microbusiness licenses often have fewer licensing fees and lower barriers to entry, making it easier for small-scale entrepreneurs to enter the cannabis industry.

4. Flexibility: Microbusinesses can quickly adapt to changes in consumer demand due to

their control over the production process.

Disadvantages of a Cannabis Microbusiness

1. Regulatory Challenges: Microbusinesses must comply with a range of regulations, which can be complex and time-consuming to navigate.

2. Limited Scale: Microbusiness licenses often limit the size of the operation, such as the number of plants that can be grown or the square footage of the cultivation area.

3. Financial Challenges: The cannabis industry faces high taxation rates and difficulties accessing traditional banking services, which can pose significant financial challenges.

4. Competition and Market Pressure: The cannabis industry is becoming increasingly competitive, with both industry-specific and broader economic challenges

5. High Initial Investment: Setting up a vertically integrated operation can require significant capital, which can be a barrier for small businesses.

In conclusion, while a cannabis microbusiness can offer several advantages such as control over production and a focus on local craft products, it also comes with challenges including regulatory complexities, limited scale, financial difficulties, and competitive pressures. Therefore, it's crucial for potential microbusiness owners to carefully consider these factors and plan accordingly.

Ancillary Businesses

Cannabis is a multi-billion dollar industry. A lot of newcomers assume that the only way to break into the cannabis industry is to obtain a license that involves touching the plant as we call it. But what most people don't know is that most of the early millionaires in the cannabis space back in the day did not own licenses. They were people who had ancillary businesses that supported the cannabis industry, as in not touching the plant as we call it. An analogy that was told to me back in the day was that the cannabis industry was like the gold rush back in the early 1900s. Digging for the gold and selling the gold was the equivalent of what a cannabis license is today. But the guys who set up shop along the highways headed to the gold mines that sold picks and shovels were the guys who did the least work and probably made the most money. I will never forget that at one of the first legitimate cannabis trade shows (Cannabis Business Cannabis World Expo), I attended a seminar on successful businesses in the cannabis space and one of the most successful companies at that time was a packaging company that was already traded on the NASDAQ!

Remember a non-plant touching ancillary business in the cannabis industry refers to companies that provide products or services to support the cannabis industry but do not directly grow, process, or sell cannabis products. These businesses play a crucial role in the industry's operation, growth, and compliance

1. Regulatory Compliance and Legal Services: These businesses help cannabis companies navigate the complex regulatory landscape of the cannabis industry. This can include lawyers specializing in cannabis law, compliance consultants, and companies that provide seed-to-sale tracking systems.

2. Financial Services: Due to the federal illegality of cannabis in the United States, many traditional banks shy away from the sector. As a result, some businesses specialize in

providing financial services to the cannabis industry, such as specialized lenders and payment processors.

1. Marketing and Branding Services: These businesses help cannabis companies build their brand and market their products. This can include advertising agencies, social media consultants, and packaging design firms.

2. Equipment and Technology Providers: These businesses provide the

equipment and technology needed by cannabis companies. This can include companies that manufacture cultivation equipment, companies that develop software for managing cannabis businesses, and firms that create technology for testing and quality assurance.

3. Security Services: Given the high-value nature of cannabis products and the cash-intensive nature of the industry, security services are crucial. This can include companies that provide physical security services, as well as firms that offer security technology like surveillance systems.

4. Consulting Services: These businesses provide expert advice to cannabis companies on various aspects of the industry, from cultivation techniques to business strategy.

5. Laboratory Testing: These businesses test cannabis products for potency and contaminants, ensuring they are safe for consumption.

6. Packaging: These businesses provide specialized packaging that meets the strict regulatory requirements of the cannabis industry.

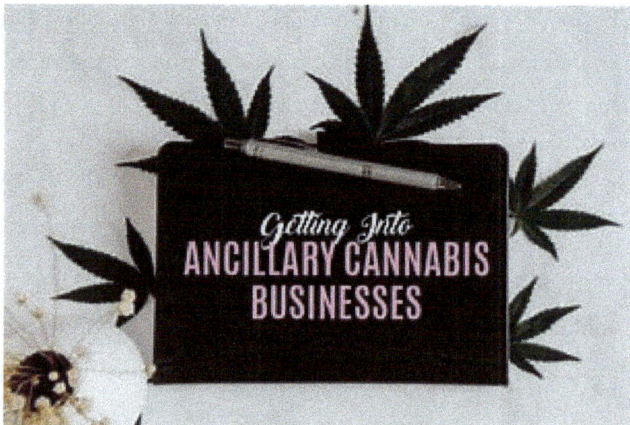

The advantages of these ancillary businesses include a lower barrier to entry compared to plant-touching businesses, as they don't have to secure a cannabis business license through a complex and costly application process. However, they still face significant regulation compared to many non-cannabis businesses. The future of the cannabis industry lies in the success of ancillary businesses. These businesses provide essential services and products that support the cannabis industry without directly touching the plant. From regulatory compliance and legal services to financial services, marketing and branding, equipment and technology, security, consulting, laboratory testing, and packaging, these businesses play a crucial role in the industry's operation, growth, and compliance. As the industry continues to expand and evolve, the demand for these services will only increase, presenting immense opportunities for innovative entrepreneurs and investors. With the continued legalization and acceptance of cannabis, more states and countries will open up to this industry, creating a global demand for ancillary businesses. As the market matures, we can expect to see increased specialization and innovation within each sector, leading to even greater profitability and growth. By focusing on ancillary businesses, entrepreneurs can tap into the lucrative cannabis market without the risks and complexities associated with obtaining a license to touch the plant. The future of the cannabis industry is bright.

Financial Management in Cannabis

In the burgeoning world of the cannabis industry, understanding the nuances of financial management is not merely an option—it's an imperative for success. As green waves of progress sweep across the United States, entrepreneurs and investors are turning their gaze to this once-taboo field, recognizing the potential for substantial economic gain. Yet, with great potential comes the need for astute planning and a firm grasp of financial fundamentals.

The lifeblood of any business is its cash flow. In the context of cannabis, where regulatory landscapes can shift and consumer trends evolve at a dizzying pace, managing cash flow becomes a high-stakes endeavor. A cannabis enterprise must anticipate expenses, from cultivation to marketing, while ensuring revenue streams are both robust and compliant with legal stipulations.

Consider the tale of Green Horizon, a pioneer in the Colorado cannabis market. They meticulously tracked their cash inflows from retail sales and outflows for production costs, yielding a transparent financial blueprint that guided their expansion. Such clarity allowed them to navigate the tumultuous early days of legalization, where others stumbled in the haze of complexity.

But cash flow is just one piece of the puzzle. Investment in the cannabis space is as much about timing as it is about money. The early movers in states like Colorado and Washington were able to capitalize on first-mover advantages, securing prime real estate and establishing brand recognition while the market was still in its nascent stage. As the industry matures, investment strategies must evolve. The savvy investor asks, "Where is the next growth opportunity? Is it in biotech innovation for strain development, or perhaps in the burgeoning field of cannabis tourism?"

To explore different perspectives, let's consider the cautious investor who is wary of the volatility inherent in the cannabis market. They might diversify their portfolio, perhaps allocating only a portion to direct cannabis operations, while investing the remainder in ancillary businesses such as security, software, or equipment that serve the industry. This approach hedges against market fluctuations while still capturing a slice of the cannabis pie.

Data and facts are critical for informed decision-making. In 2020, legal cannabis sales in the United States exceeded $17.5 billion, a 46% increase from the previous year. This meteoric rise illustrates the market's potential but also underscores the importance of astute financial management to navigate such explosive growth.

Complex terms like "280E tax code" can confound even the most experienced businessperson. It's essential to clarify that this part of the U.S. tax code forbids cannabis companies from deducting ordinary business expenses due to the federal illegality of cannabis. This impacts how businesses in the industry manage their finances, often leading to higher effective tax rates and necessitating creative (yet legal) accounting strategies to optimize tax burdens.

As you ponder these insights, ask yourself: How will you chart your financial course in the cannabis industry? Will you be the daring pioneer or the cautious navigator? Either way, may your journey be as fruitful as the very plants at the heart of this economic revolution. In the ever-evolving world of the cannabis industry, the next chapter promises both exciting opportunities and challenges. As legalization continues to expand across more states and countries, the market is set to experience exponential growth. However, with this growth comes increased competition and regulatory scrutiny. Entrepreneurs and investors must stay ahead of the curve by embracing innovation and adaptability, while also maintaining a keen awareness of financial management strategies. This includes diligent cash flow management, strategic investment decisions, and a thorough understanding of the unique tax implications in the cannabis industry. It is a thrilling time for those brave enough to venture into this uncharted territory, where fortunes can be made or lost. By staying informed, being proactive, and approaching the industry with a blend of creativity and caution, individuals can carve out their own success stories in the ever-expanding world of cannabis. The future holds endless possibilities, and the only limit is one's imagination and willingness to adapt to the winds of change.

In conclusion, mastering financial management in the cannabis industry is akin to navigating a labyrinth. One must be nimble, informed, and strategic, always anticipating the next turn. Key takeaways include the critical nature of cash flow management, the importance of timing and research in investment, and the necessity of understanding the unique tax implications of the cannabis trade. With these insights, a cannabis entrepreneur or investor is better equipped to reap the lucrative rewards that this green frontier offers.

Compliance and Legal Updates

In the rapidly evolving landscape of the cannabis industry, staying current with compliance and legal updates is not just a matter of due diligence—it is a survival imperative. The history of cannabis regulation in the United States is a tapestry woven with controversy, reform, and a burgeoning recognition of the plant's economic potential.

From the earliest days of prohibition to the current wave of legalization, cannabis has been subject to intense legal scrutiny and regulation. It began with the Marihuana Tax Act of 1937, which effectively criminalized cannabis, casting a shadow over its use and distribution for decades. This regulatory chokehold was tightened with the Controlled Substances Act of 1970, branding cannabis as a Schedule I drug, alongside heroin and LSD, deemed to have a high potential for abuse and no accepted medical use.

However, the winds of change began to stir in the 1990s. California's Proposition 215 in 1996 marked a historic milestone—the first state law legalizing medical cannabis. This revolutionary act set the stage for an incremental, yet relentless march toward legalization across the country.

As you leaf through the pages of this historical journey, consider the images that mark these turning points: a newspaper clipping announcing the passage of Proposition 215, a photograph of the first legally purchased recreational cannabis in Colorado, and diagrams of state-by-state legalization statuses. Each visual is a testament to the industry's dynamic trajectory.

The cultural and regional variations in cannabis legalization are telling. Some states, like Colorado and Washington, emerged as pioneers, fully embracing both medical and recreational legalization. In contrast, others have taken a more conservative approach, either decriminalizing possession or allowing only medical use. These disparities create a patchwork of regulations that businesses must navigate with precision and foresight.

Fast forward to the present, and we are witnessing an industry that is rapidly adapting to new opportunities and challenges. The landmark 2018 Farm Bill, which legalized hemp by removing it from the definition of marijuana under the Controlled Substances Act, has opened doors for the production of CBD products, further complicating the regulatory landscape.

But with progress comes growing pains. The ever-changing state and federal laws create a labyrinth of compliance requirements that can confound even the most diligent of businesses. For instance, the introduction of the SAFE Banking Act aims to address the

financial services hurdles faced by cannabis companies, yet its passage remains uncertain, leaving many to operate in a cash-heavy, risk-laden environment.

Have you ever pondered the precarious position of a business operating legally on a state level but still considered illegal federally? This dichotomy is the root of many challenges, from banking to taxation, and highlights the ongoing controversy surrounding cannabis.

Hopefully with President Biden's latest opinion on rescheduling cannabis will be the end of cannabis prohibition in the United States.

As a cannabis entrepreneur, you must be vigilant, constantly monitoring the shifting sands of legislation. Significant controversies, such as the debate over the potency of cannabis products or the inclusion of social equity programs in legalization efforts, can rapidly alter the course of business operations.

Navigating this complex legal terrain requires not just adherence to existing laws but also an anticipatory stance toward potential changes. Stay informed, adapt swiftly, and always, always remain compliant. Your business—and indeed, your fortune—depends on it.

Remember this: In the realm of the cannabis industry, where the only constant is change, your ability to remain compliant and legally astute is not just a strategy—it's the very essence of your success.

CHAPTER THREE

MAKING THAT DOUGH: FINANCIAL STRATEGIES

Funding Your Cannabis Empire

Securing funding may be one of the biggest obstacles that a cannabis entrepreneur faces. I know plenty of people who have gone through the entire process of doing all the research, finding locations, securing a license, finding a team of individuals who are ready to work, have jumped through all the zoning hurdles and are ready to go but because this is a schedule one drug, there is no financing through a regular bank. In the regular business world, all you need is a good business plan, some initial money, and a location and usually, you're in business and a bank would freely do business with you.

Unfortunately, banking is still a major issue when it comes to the cannabis industry. Because of that, the only options are to seek private investors or Angel investors which could make you and your business vulnerable to equity encroachment. Because most of the private lenders know that you don't have the option of going to a bank for financing, they take advantage of that. They either ask for an absorbent amount of equity or very high-interest rates in return for their investments. After the rules passed here in California and licenses were handed out, along with the new licenses and rules, came lots of compliance and regulations that we all had to follow. Well, one of the unfortunate issues with rules and regulations within the cannabis space is that it is expensive to get yourself into compliance when you don't have access to capital. As I mentioned earlier, social equity applicants were given somewhat of a leg up to get into the industry, but because of a lack of financing, most of them were not able to get going. I have been working with several social equity awardees in the state of Illinois but because of a lack of funding, we are still going on a year or two of trying to find locations and getting equipment financing just to get into business. So my suggestion is to have a source of finances lined up for your business venture. It is important to scale your business plan down to the bare minimum just so that you can get your business open. Fortunately, as it sits in this country at the moment, cannabis still is a Schedule One substance and not everyone can get a license so profits are still very high. That being said, if you can get your business up and going, there's a high probability that you can get into the black very soon in a capped market that doesn't have issues with an over-saturation of cannabis businesses. As I said earlier securing funding for a cannabis business can be challenging due to the federal illegality of cannabis in the United States, which makes traditional banks and financial institutions hesitant to provide loans or other financial services. However, there are several ways to secure funding for cannabis businesses.

1. Private Investors: Private investors, including venture capital funds, angel investors, and cannabis business consulting firms, have become a significant source of funding for cannabis businesses. These investors typically require businesses to have a solid business plan, be in compliance with state law, and provide monthly and annual gross sales figures.

2. Crowdfunding: Crowdfunding platforms like Indiegogo and Kickstarter can be a viable option for cannabis businesses. These platforms allow businesses to present their business plans and attract small investments from a large number of people.

3. Debt Financing: This involves borrowing money from a lender and agreeing to pay it back with interest. While traditional banks may be hesitant to provide loans to cannabis businesses, some credit unions and private loan issuers offer high-interest loans to cannabis businesses.

4. Equity Financing: This involves selling a stake in your business to investors in exchange for capital. This can be a good option for businesses that are willing to share ownership and profits with investors.

5. Reinvesting Profits: If your business is already profitable, you can reinvest your profits back into the business to fund growth.

6. Supplier Cash Advances and Equipment Financing: Some suppliers offer cash advances or equipment financing to businesses, which can be a good option for businesses that need to purchase equipment or inventory.

7. Investments from Friends and Family: Some cannabis businesses secure funding from friends and family. However, this should be approached with caution to avoid potential personal conflicts.

8. Specialized Cannabis Lenders: Some lenders specialize in providing loans to cannabis businesses. These lenders understand the unique challenges and opportunities in the cannabis industry and may be more willing to provide funding.

When seeking funding, it's important to have a well-outlined business plan, thoroughly documented accounting records, and a clear commitment to compliance and ethical practices. It's also crucial to understand the unique regulations that make your company compliant and be ready to reinvest in essential equipment.

Revenue Streams and Diversification

As the dawn of legalization broke across the United States, a verdant opportunity sprouted for entrepreneurs and visionaries alike: the cannabis industry. Here, amidst this burgeoning field, lies an intricate lattice of potential revenue streams, each ripe for cultivation. Yet, without the proper guidance, one might find themselves lost in a maze of economic pitfalls, with their dreams of prosperity withering on the vine.

The primary issue at hand is the lack of diversification in the revenue channels of many cannabis businesses. All too often, there is an over-reliance on a single aspect of the market—be it cultivation, retail, or ancillary services. This tunnel vision can lead to vulnerability; a shift in legislation, market saturation, or a simple change in consumer preference could spell disaster for the undiversified enterprise.

Should such scenarios unfold, the consequences are dire. Businesses may see their profit margins evaporate like mist in the morning sun. Jobs could be uprooted, and the hard-earned progress of industry pioneers could crumble to dust. The domino effect of these consequences could even reverberate beyond individual companies, stunting the growth of the industry at large.

But let us not dwell on the shadows of what might be. Instead, let us turn our faces towards the light of a solution—a strategic diversification of revenue streams. By not putting all our eggs in one basket, we create a robust business model that can weather the inevitable storms of a fluctuating market.

To implement this strategy, one must first conduct a comprehensive analysis of the market, identifying various opportunities that align with the company's core competencies and values. This could involve branching into the realms of edibles and topicals, investing in research and development for medicinal uses, or expanding into the digital space with apps and platforms that support the cannabis community.

As the wheels of this strategy begin to turn, evidence of its efficacy emerges. Take, for instance, the story of Green Horizons, a company once teetering on the brink of collapse due to an oversaturated local market for flower products. By diversifying into the production of CBD-infused skincare and forging partnerships with wellness centers, they not only salvaged their business but tripled their revenue within two years.

But what of other solutions? Some advocate for mergers and acquisitions as a means to consolidate market share and resources. While this can indeed be a viable path for some, it also carries the risk of homogenizing the industry and stifling innovation. Others suggest a focus on hyper-specialization, becoming the unquestioned expert in a narrow field. This too has merit but does not safeguard against the volatility of consumer trends.

What then, dear reader, would you do if faced with the choice of diversifying or deepening your niche? Can you see the wisdom in spreading your seeds far and wide, ensuring that some will find fertile ground, no matter the season?

It is through such direct questions that we engage not only the mind but the spirit of entrepreneurship. Imagine a tapestry woven with strands of gold, silver, and silk. Each thread represents a different revenue stream—resilient alone, but together, an unbreakable weave of success.

And so, we must not be sparing in our endeavors. Let the potency of our verbs and the solidity of our nouns paint the picture of a thriving cannabis business, one that stands tall and unyielding amidst the ever-shifting sands of commerce.

For emphasis, it is crucial to remember that diversification is not merely a strategy; it is a safeguard against the unpredictability of tomorrow.

In the words of a seasoned cultivator, "To survive in this industry, you must be as adaptable as the plant we cherish. Diversify, and let your business flourish in ways you never thought possible."

Thus, we see that by showing—not telling—the power of diversification through real-world examples and engaging storytelling, we can inspire a new generation of cannabis entrepreneurs to build their empires on a foundation of resilience and foresight. Let's navigate the volatile path to making millions in the cannabis industry.

Navigating Taxation in Cannabis

Whenever I speak at tradeshows across the country I am amused by the faces of the audience when we get on the subject of taxes. There is usually a face of disbelief. I think it is atrocious how we are taxed in this industry. I also believe it is one of the main reasons that licensed cannabis businesses go rogue.

In the lush fields of the cannabis industry, a daunting obstacle often looms large: taxation. As one of the first cannabis businesses in the United States, we've navigated through the thicket of tax laws that are as complex and shifting as the strains of the plants we cultivate. In this chapter, we aim to demystify the unique tax implications for cannabis businesses and offer strategies to manage them effectively.

To set the stage, let us first understand that cannabis, while legal for medicinal and

recreational use in several states remains a Schedule I controlled substance at the federal level. This classification carries significant tax repercussions, particularly stemming from the Internal Revenue Code Section 280E, which prohibits businesses dealing in controlled substances from deducting ordinary business expenses. The immediate question arises: How can a cannabis business thrive when faced with such an onerous tax code?

Delving deeper, let's explore the concept of 'Cost of Goods Sold' (COGS), the one deduction Section 280E permits. COGS includes the direct costs attributable to the production of the products sold by a company. Cannabis companies can include costs such as seeds, soil, and labor directly related to cultivation. However, the line between what qualifies as COGS and what does not can often blur, leaving businesses to walk a tightrope between compliance and optimization.

Consider, for instance, a case study involving Green Essence, a pioneering cannabis dispensary. Initially, Green Essence was not maximizing its COGS deductions, leaving a sizable portion of potential tax savings unclaimed. After consulting with tax experts who specialized in the cannabis industry, they restructured their accounting practices to clearly define and document all direct production costs. As a result, their taxable income significantly decreased, leading to substantial tax savings.

Different perspectives on this matter reveal a spectrum of strategies. Some businesses take a conservative approach, deducting only the bare minimum to avoid the ire of the Internal Revenue Service (IRS). Others adopt a more aggressive stance, interpreting the tax code in a way that maximizes deductions. This high-risk, high-reward strategy can either result in greater profitability or invite rigorous audits and penalties.

Facts and data underscore the importance of getting taxation right. For example, the average effective federal tax rate for cannabis businesses can hover around 70%, compared to 21% for other businesses after the Tax Cuts and Jobs Act of 2017. Such a disparity is not merely a footnote; it is a chasm that can swallow profits whole.

When discussing complex terms such as 'Section 280E' or 'COGS', it is imperative to clarify that these are not mere buzzwords but pivotal elements in the financial lexicon of the cannabis entrepreneur. Section 280E, for example, is the sword of Damocles hanging over every transaction, every expansion, and every innovation in the cannabis space.

As we draw this discussion to its close, let us harvest the key takeaways. Taxation in the cannabis industry is a labyrinthine challenge, fraught with pitfalls and traps for the unwary. Yet, with astute management and strategic planning, it is possible to navigate these treacherous waters.

Have you, dear reader, considered how taxation could impact your cannabis venture? Would your strategy emphasize caution or boldness? How would you ensure that the lifeblood of your business—its profits—are not unduly siphoned by the taxman?

Let this be the one-sentence paragraph that resonates with you: In the realm of cannabis taxation, knowledge is not just power—it is profit.

In conclusion, while the path to millions in the cannabis industry is lined with the promise of green, it is also shadowed by the complexities of taxation. To tread this path

successfully, one must be as shrewd as a tax attorney and as innovative as a master cultivator. In the words of an industry veteran, "Understanding taxation is like understanding the soil; it's what everything else grows from."

By providing a clear, comprehensive guide with vivid imagery and engaging questions, this chapter aims to equip you with the tools to make informed decisions about your cannabis business's financial future. Remember, it's not just about how much you make— it's about how much you keep. Show the IRS the respect it commands, but do not let fear stunt the growth of your ambitions

Financial Forecasting and Metrics

Embarking on a journey through the verdant fields of the cannabis industry, one must cultivate not only the finest plants but also the sturdiest financial forecasts and metrics. They are the trellis that supports the thriving growth of your business, guiding you upwards toward the sunlight of success. In this vital chapter, we shall delve into the art and science of developing robust financial models and key performance indicators (KPIs) for your cannabis enterprise.

Your goal, as the architect of your business's financial future, is to create a dynamic and responsive financial model that informs your decision-making and propels you toward your goal of making millions. With precision and foresight, you can anticipate the ebb and flow of the market, sidestep potential pitfalls, and seize opportunities with the confidence of a seasoned pioneer.

To achieve this, you require several tools in your financial toolkit: historical financial data, market research, a deep understanding of your operational costs, and the ability to project future scenarios. These are your seeds, soil, and water, the very essentials for nurturing your financial garden.

Let us first cast a gaze upon the broad landscape. At its heart, financial forecasting for your cannabis business involves projecting sales, costs, and profits into the future. These projections are the map by which you'll navigate the uncertain terrain of the industry. But before we journey down the path of intricate details, it's essential to understand the importance of KPIs. These are the signposts that keep you on course, ensuring that every step you take moves you closer to your ultimate destination.

Now, let us delve into the intricate roots and stems of our financial garden. Begin by estimating your sales forecast. How many customers do you anticipate, and at what average purchase amount? Calculate the growth rate based on market trends and your business strategy. Remember, sales are the rain that nourishes your business, but overestimation is the storm that could flood your aspirations.

Next, consider the cost of goods sold (COGS). It's the amount of water required for each plant, and the nutrients for each bud. This includes the cost of cultivating, harvesting, and processing your cannabis. COGS directly affects your gross margin – the healthier it is, the more robust your business will be.

After COGS, account for your operating expenses. From the rent of your dispensary to the wages of your knowledgeable staff, these are the supporting stakes and ties that give

shape to your business. Ensure you understand the fixed and variable nature of each expense, as they will fluctuate with the scale of your operation.

Be mindful of the adage: "A stitch in time saves nine." Offer practical advice to the reader; keep a reserve for unexpected costs or changes in regulation. Stay flexible and adaptive, like the wise plant that bends with the wind rather than breaking.

For testing or validation, compare your financial projections with actual performance. Regularly update your model with real-world data to maintain its relevance and accuracy. If the numbers begin to diverge significantly, it's time to prune and adjust.

In the event of discrepancies, troubleshooting becomes your ally. If sales are lower than expected, investigate whether it's due to decreased foot traffic, pricing, or product quality. If costs are higher, consider whether there are efficiencies you can introduce or if supplier negotiations are in order.

Let's take a moment to pause and reflect. Have you considered the potential financial outcomes for your business? What if the market shifts unexpectedly, or a new competitor emerges? How will your financial model stand up to the test of these real-world challenges?

The rhythm of your business, like the cadence of this text, should be steady yet adaptable, ready to quicken when the opportunity arises or to slow down when caution is warranted. Use strong verbs and nouns to describe the actions you'll take – forecast, analyze, optimize, and innovate.

Remember, your financial projections are not just dry data; they are the lifeblood of your enterprise. They tell a story of where you've been and illuminate the path to where you're going. Use vivid imagery to bring this data to life: Picture your sales forecast as a rising sun, your COGS as the fertile soil, and your operating expenses as the diligent gardeners tending to the growth.

In conclusion, the creation of financial forecasts and metrics is akin to charting a course through an unexplored wilderness. It requires skill, foresight, and the courage to venture into the unknown. As you turn each page, let the lessons herein be the compass that guides you, the map that leads you, and the lamp that lights your way through the dense forest of financial planning. With this knowledge, the lucrative harvest of the cannabis industry awaits you.

Exit Strategies and ROI

In the bustling marketplace of the cannabis industry, amid the hum of innovation and the aroma of opportunity, there lies a stark reality that every entrepreneur must face: the future sale or transition of their business. It is the eventual junction where dreams are either solidified into lasting legacies or quietly fade away.

In a world where the only constant is change, the question arises: what becomes of your cannabis enterprise when it's time to turn the page? The path you've trodden has been lined with the verdant promise of growth and the golden potential of profit. You've nurtured your business from seedling to full bloom, but now, you must consider the harvest of your hard work: the exit strategy. The absence of a well-considered exit strategy is akin to navigating a ship without a compass. Should storms arise, or winds change, without a plan, your vessel could be dashed against unforeseen rocks. The consequences? Diminished returns, lost investments, or even the total collapse of the empire you've meticulously built.

The solution blooms in the form of preparation and foresight. Begin by evaluating the most suitable exit options. Will you pass the torch through a sale, a merger, or perhaps an acquisition? Could a partnership be the key to unlocking the door to your next venture, or might it be more prudent to let public investors take the reins through an initial public offering (IPO)? Implementing this strategy requires a series of calculated steps. First, ensure your financials are impeccable, as they are the bedrock upon which buyers will base their valuations. Next, streamline your operations to showcase a business running at peak efficiency. Then, engage with legal and financial advisors to navigate the complexities of a business transition.

Evidence of success lies in the tales of those who came before you. Look to industry veterans who have sold their businesses for a substantial profit. Their journeys are replete with lessons on timing, negotiation, and valuation – critical components that turned their exit strategies into legendary industry benchmarks. While the allure of a lucrative sale is strong, consider the alternative solutions. Some entrepreneurs choose to retain a stake in the business, offering their expertise as consultants while enjoying the fruits of passive income. Others opt for a gradual handover, training successors to maintain the business's legacy.

Reflect now, for a moment. How will you measure the true value of the empire you've built? Consider the Return on Investment (ROI). It's more than just a metric; it's the story of your journey, the quantification of risk and reward, the tangible expression of your strategic acumen. ROI in the cannabis industry is not merely calculated on spreadsheets but grown through the nurturing of relationships, the cultivation of a brand, and the harvest of customer loyalty. To optimize your ROI, align your business with emerging market trends, diversify your offerings, and endeavor to create a brand that resonates deeply with your customers. Calculating your ROI should be approached with the same meticulous care as cultivating your finest strain. Consider not only the direct financial gains but also the intangible assets you've developed: brand reputation, intellectual property, and market share.

As you ponder these points, ask yourself: Are you ready for what the future holds? Are you prepared to take the steps necessary to ensure that the exit from your cannabis enterprise is as successful as its inception? Bring to your exit strategy the same creativity and resilience that you've applied to every other aspect of your business. Let the rhythm of your planning be both deliberate and dynamic, a testament to the pioneering spirit that has brought you this far.

In conclusion, remember that the sale or transition of your business is not the end but rather a metamorphosis. It is the moment when the seeds of your labor blossom into the enduring legacy of your entrepreneurial spirit. With careful planning, strategic decision-making, and an eye on ROI, you can ensure that this final chapter is written on your terms, securing your place in the annals of the cannabis industry's pioneers.

CHAPTER FOUR

BIGGEST KEY TO SUCCESS: MARKETING AND BRANDING

Crafting a Compelling Brand Story

O ut of all the advice that I have given in this book I think branding and marketing are the two most important things you must do to make millions within this industry. As with any industry, branding, and marketing is very important, but in the cannabis industry, it is paramount. Because cannabis is more of a culture than a product that you sell. When you look at superstars within the entertainment world, a lot of them have product lines that they put out, because people tend to like familiarity and associating products with people. So popular people who have products within the industry usually that have a successful acting or singing career, usually do well. Because cannabis is more of a cultural thing, people tend to lean towards supporting products that come from people or organizations that they feel are true to cannabis culture. Take Rihanna the singer for instance, because she is a beautiful, sexy individual who carries herself with class and grace when she came out with her product lines, it translated immediately because of the way that she carries herself and the products that she was promoting which are beauty and lingerie products.

This can be said within the cannabis industry as well. Athletes or mainly music artists, especially in the hip-hop industry, do really well with products that are branded in their names. If you look at one of the most recognizable brands in the industry, which is the Cookies brand, you can see a direct correlation to the culture and the following that this brand has because of the artists that this company associates itself. Despite the many rumored issues that this company has the brand is still very strong. There are instances within this industry, where someone outside of the culture has tried to team up with someone from the culture and sell products, and it doesn't go well at all. As I said, the cannabis industry is a culture and the people in this culture protect it and they don't like corporate or outsiders coming in to cash in on its popularity. I remember meeting with a very rich corporate group that took over the Marley brand in the beginning. I warned these "suits", as I called them, that they were not going to be able to buy their way into the industry by grabbing a licensing deal with arguably the most popular Cannabis smoking person that ever lived which is Bob Marley. I was told that and I'm paraphrasing, "We are corporate guys... We made millions of dollars running major businesses. I think we can handle this industry ". All I can say is boy were they wrong because as soon as they tried to come out, the cannabis culture ate them alive for being a bunch of corporate suits, not caring about the brand or the quality of the product that they put out and the industry took offense to it as they were disgracing a national icon. I say all of this to say that branding is everything in this industry. If you want to become popular and make sales, I'm not saying that an outsider can't come into the industry, but they have to be very strategic in connecting with someone "of" the industry and being a good player within the culture. I have been offered numerous contracts, and even been in a few lawsuits with some bad players, because they only wanted to use me because of my influence and ties to the pioneering of this industry. I learned my lessons on that and I would advise anyone to evaluate, do your due diligence, and look into anyone that you may pick up as a partner. Money isn't everything and as they say "all money is in good money", so be careful who you partner with.

I have a couple of brands that I started and I even created a brand called Hip-Hop Legacy Brands, of which I teamed up with some hip-hop royalty and my brand is doing well. At the moment I have several hip-hop legacy brand stores in the country of Thailand. Because hip-hop is such a big part of the cannabis culture, my brands are doing excellent in that country.

Advertising is crucial to getting your product sold in any industry, but this industry really connects with social media platforms. My advice to anyone seeking to get into this industry and wanting to know how to promote their brands would be to definitely get your brands on the social media platforms in the correct way so that you can advertise heavily to them within whatever rules they have in place. There are many other ways to brand your product and advertise more traditionally - you can check out some of those below as well:

1. Differentiation: A strong brand helps a cannabis business stand out in a competitive market. It differentiates the business from competitors and can own a word or phrase in consumers' minds.

2. Customer Acquisition and Retention: Effective branding and marketing strategies can attract and retain customers, driving sales and fostering customer loyalty.

3. Trust and Reputation: Quality branding and consistent messaging can build trust with consumers, which is essential in the evolving cannabis industry.

4. Regulatory Compliance: Given the complex legal environment surrounding the cannabis industry, branding and marketing must comply with all applicable laws and regulations.

5. Education: Branding and marketing can be used to educate consumers about different cannabis strains, products, and responsible consumption.

6. Investor Attraction: A strong brand can attract investment, making the business more valuable.

The best ways to brand and market in the cannabis space include:

1. Understanding Your Audience: Know your target audience's demographics, preferences, and values, and create a brand that speaks to their needs and desires.

2. Storytelling: Craft a compelling brand story that conveys your company's mission, values, and history. This creates a connection between your brand and consumers, making your company more relatable and memorable.

3. Quality and Consistency: Offer top-quality products and maintain consistency in your branding. This includes logos, packaging, and marketing materials.

4. SEO and Digital Marketing: Utilize search engine optimization and digital marketing strategies to increase your online visibility and reach more potential customers.

5. Influencer Marketing: Partner with influencers who have a genuine interest in the cannabis industry, a strong and engaged following, and

a history of posting authentic, high-quality content.

6. Educational Content: Present educational content to create trust and brand recognition with your consumer base, particularly those who are new to cannabis products.

7. Authenticity: Highlight the authenticity of your products, cultivation practices, and commitment to quality.

8. Regulatory Compliance: Stay current with the ever-changing cannabis regulations in your state and ensure your branding complies with local laws.

In summary, effective branding and marketing are essential for success in the cannabis industry. They help differentiate a business, attract and retain customers, build trust, comply with regulations, educate consumers, and attract investment. The best strategies involve understanding your audience, storytelling, maintaining quality and consistency, utilizing SEO and digital marketing, partnering with influencers, presenting educational content, highlighting authenticity, and complying with regulations.

Navigating Advertising Restrictions

I had to learn the hard way on this topic! I was once heavily fined by the city of Los Angeles because of signage at my dispensary. There was nothing I could do but pay the bill because I failed to read up on the local law regarding signage within the city limits.

As a cannabis pioneer, this brings back memories of when you could not even advertise anywhere back when we opened some of the first businesses. I remember the only place that I could advertise was the back of the LA Weekly near the porn section for crying out loud!

In an era of burgeoning enterprise and innovation, the cannabis industry stands as a testament to the American spirit of entrepreneurialism. Yet, amidst the green rush, a significant hurdle casts a shadow on the luminous path to prosperity: the stringent web of advertising restrictions, a remnant of an age-old stigma surrounding this versatile plant. It is within this complex landscape that cannabis pioneers must learn to navigate, or risk the peril of obscurity in an increasingly competitive market.

The primary issue here is clear: a labyrinth of legal constraints severely limits how cannabis businesses can market their products. Federal laws, inconsistent state regulations, and platform-specific policies create a minefield for any marketer daring to promote cannabis. What is at stake if this challenge goes unaddressed? Well, imagine the potential of a seed that never sprouts, a brand that never finds its audience and a message that fades before it can even echo. The consequences, simply put, could spell disaster for businesses that fail to adapt, potentially stifling the growth of the entire industry.

But where there is a challenge, there is also opportunity. The solution lies in creativity and compliance, a dual-edged sword to carve a path through the thicket of restrictions. One must first understand the rules to bend them to one's advantage. This means keeping abreast of the ever-shifting legal landscape, engaging with legal counsel, and devising advertising strategies that are as innovative as they are compliant.

Implementing this approach begins with education. Business owners need to be versed in the nuances of the law, understanding the distinction between what is prohibited and what is merely discouraged. From there, it's about crafting a narrative that resonates with the target audience without crossing any legal boundaries. This could involve leveraging the power of educational content, harnessing the influence of brand ambassadors, or exploring the untapped potential of experiential marketing.

Evidence of the efficacy of such strategies is not merely anecdotal. Take, for instance, the success of businesses that have turned to content marketing, providing value through educational blogs, and informative videos that subtly highlight their products. Not only does this foster trust and authority, but it also circumvents traditional advertising channels that are often off-limits.

Yet, even as some navigate these treacherous waters with aplomb, alternative solutions beckon. Why not consider grassroots campaigns that rally the community and create a groundswell of organic support? Or strategic partnerships with non-cannabis brands that share similar values? These avenues, while less direct, can build a brand's presence in the public consciousness without confrontation with the law.

The road ahead is anything but smooth. Still, consider this: what if the very restrictions

we bemoan are the crucible from which more authentic and innovative marketing is born? Could it be that, in the end, these limitations are a blessing in disguise, compelling us to market in ways that forge deeper connections with our audience?

In the dance of words and imagery that marketers perform, the goal is never merely to sell; it is to tell a story that captivates and resonates. The cannabis industry has a particularly poignant tale, one of resilience, healing, and hope. So, let us ask ourselves: How can we best share this story within the confines of the law?

The answers may not come easily, but by embracing the constraints, we encourage a level of creativity that might never have been tapped otherwise. Remember, a well-tended garden cares not for the fence that surrounds it, so long as the gardener knows how to make the most of the space within. Let us then tend to our businesses with the same philosophy, crafting marketing strategies that not only abide by the rules but elevate our brands to new heights. With a blend of creativity, compliance, and courage, we can navigate the advertising restrictions and emerge not just unscathed, but triumphant.

Social Media and Community Engagement

One of the biggest and often overlooked ways of advertising your business is social media. I remember back in 2003 when there was no real social media. The only way I had to advertise my workout gym/tanning salon was through this little magazine called The Penny Saver. It was a small paper brochure that was usually given out for free, but to advertise even in the smallest area. Still was a couple hundred bucks per week, and that's a lot of money when you're just starting out. Also hiring a publicist or an advertising firm is very expensive and most of them didn't want to touch cannabis in the first place. But now the social media platforms are warming up to cannabis, even though they don't still allow you to sell or truly promote a THC-based product, they are much more cannabis- friendly than when I first started. I remember setting up my Dispensary and Clone department on social media and had several thousand followers. Then one day a competitor started to come to my page and leave a bunch of negative comments so we found out and blocked this person. Then this person, appley contacted Twitter and Instagram and brought attention to my page and they completely shut me down and I lost literally thousands and thousands of followers that I worked hard to get. Over the years I built a following and every once in a while, my page would be removed. So nowadays, it is very important to understand the rules of social media, and be very smart and how you advertise there. With the advance of social media, influencers, and alike, and the potential of something going, viral, social media seems to be one of the main ways of advertising and building a brand these days.

In the verdant world of the cannabis industry, where every brand vies for the spotlight, the potency of a robust online presence and a tightly-knit community cannot be overstated. As the tendrils of social media reach into every corner of our lives, they offer a fertile ground for the cultivation of a brand that not only thrives but resonates deeply with its audience.

Imagine the early days of my journey, when the digital landscape was as untamed as the perceptions of cannabis. The setting was raw—a vista of opportunity amid the wilderness of the World Wide Web. In this new age, we saw the potential for growth where others saw barren soil. The central figures of this narrative were my brand and its loyal following—both nascent but eager to flourish. We were pioneers in a digital arena, just as we had been in the tangible world of cannabis retail and activism. The problem was clear: how to elevate our brand above the noise of a crowded internet and foster a community of dedicated enthusiasts and customers.

Our approach was holistic, rooted in authenticity, and driven by the desire to connect. We crafted our digital identity with meticulous care, ensuring that every post, every tweet, and every image was infused with the spirit of our mission. We spoke not only of our products but of our journey, our advocacy, and our dreams for the future of cannabis. The results were tangible. Followers grew into the thousands, then tens of thousands, each new member a testimony to the resonance of our message. Engagement metrics soared, with shares, likes, and comments painting a vivid picture of a thriving community.

But what did these numbers mean? Beyond the analytics, there was a deeper impact. Real conversations were happening, stories were shared, and a sense of belonging was fostered. Our brand had become a beacon, a gathering place for those who shared our passion for cannabis and its myriad benefits. Reflecting on this journey, the insights gleaned were invaluable. We learned that transparency breeds trust, engagement fosters loyalty, and content should always be as educational as it is compelling. There were, of course, criticisms—the occasional misstep in tone or choice of content—but these too were growth opportunities, reminding us that the digital world is ever-evolving and demanding of our adaptability.

Visual aids, such as infographics depicting the growth of our community and the reach of our message, served to underscore the success of our endeavors. They also provided a blueprint for others seeking to emulate our approach, a testament to the power of social media when wielded with care and strategy. Our story, however, is but a single thread in the vast tapestry of the cannabis industry's evolution. It is a narrative of change, innovation, and the relentless pursuit of connection in an age where digital presence is as critical as the quality of the product itself.

And so, dear reader, we return to the broader question: How can your brand harness the power of social media and community engagement to not only survive but thrive? How can you turn your followers into advocates, your customers into a community, and your digital presence into a legacy? The path forward may not be simple, but it is marked by the footsteps of those who have ventured before. Consider this: In a world where every like, every share and every comment is a seed planted, what kind of garden will you cultivate? Will you nurture each interaction, tend to your digital ecosystem, and reap the harvest of a community truly engaged?

As 2024 is upon us, understand that social media is the new platform for advertising and marketing. So learn the nuances and the rules so that you and your brand can take full advantage of it!

Customer Loyalty and Retention

When you are a business owner, you have a natural tendency not to trust anyone else to run the business and you feel that you are the only one who can do the job correctly. Well, as a business owner and pioneer in the cannabis space, it went beyond who you could trust to do the job, this was a business that involved the distribution of a Schedule One drug. There's jail time associated with doing something wrong in this line of business. So in the beginning as a full-time activist, a full-time entrepreneur, and someone who really understood the cannabis industry I was too afraid to let go of the leash in my business. It took about 12 years before I felt comfortable enough in the industry to hire a manager and let them run my Dispensary. I always felt that I would feel so bad if one of my employees had to endure a raid which was very common back in the days in California when we were establishing the cannabis industry. The reason I mentioned all of this is to say that by being there so long and being in a nice affluent city like Studio City California, where the celebrities and the studios are, people were very finicky about talking or dealing with anyone but me after being there so long. Your bud-tenders, security guards, and anyone who comes in contact with patients or customers must make them feel safe and welcome. Because doctors can't necessarily write prescriptions but they could write recommendations, back at the time it was important for the budtenders to know what they were talking about because they took on the role of a pharmacist. So having a safe clean location and a knowledgeable staff was paramount in customer retention.

Creating enduring customer loyalty and retention is akin to nurturing a garden; it requires careful planning, patient tending, and a deep understanding of the ecosystem. Within the burgeoning cannabis industry, where the green leaves of opportunity are ever-expanding, the goal is to cultivate a customer base that not only blooms but thrives through repeat engagements and fervent word-of-mouth.

To achieve this, one must have fertile soil – that is, a solid foundation of customer service and a high-quality product offering. In addition, a robust CRM system, a loyalty program framework, and staff trained in customer engagement and retention techniques are crucial prerequisites. With these in place, you're ready to sow the seeds of loyalty. Picture a journey where each step is a thoughtful gesture toward securing customer allegiance. This odyssey starts with an overarching view: design a loyalty program, train your staff in its intricacies, engage with customers through personalized experiences, and continuously refine the process based on feedback and market trends.

Embarking on the detailed steps, begin by designing a loyalty program that resonates with your clientele. Consider tiered rewards that entice customers to reach higher levels of spending for greater benefits. Simultaneously, train your team to recognize and appreciate regular customers, making them feel valued with every interaction. Practical advice is essential, like understanding the fine line between persuasive and pushy, or the art of personalization without invading privacy. Warn against complacency; the competition is always just a puff of smoke away.

To test the potency of your loyalty stratagems, monitor metrics such as repeat purchase rates, average transaction values, and program enrollment numbers. Observe the vibrancy in your customer community, the enthusiasm in their reviews, and the frequency of their visits. Should you encounter stumbling blocks, such as a plateau in loyalty sign-ups or a downturn in repeat visits, reassess your program's perks and communication strategy. A common pitfall is failing to keep the rewards fresh and relevant, which can often be remedied by soliciting and implementing customer feedback. Now, let's delve deeper.

Imagine walking into a dispensary where the air is perfumed with the promise of quality and the staff greet you by name, already aware of your preferences. This isn't just a transaction; it's an experience, a ritual that becomes part of the customer's lifestyle. Your loyalty program isn't a card they carry; it's a badge of honor, a membership to an exclusive club. But how do you create this atmosphere? It begins with educating your staff. They are the cultivators in your garden of loyalty. Train them to understand not just the products they're selling but also the art of reading customers and tailoring experiences. They should know when to offer advice, when to share a story, or when to simply listen.

What's your soil's pH level? In business terms, how well do you know your customer base? Collect data – responsibly and with consent – to understand buying habits, preferences, and desires. Use this to personalize interactions and to shape the rewards of your loyalty program. Do you remember the last time you felt truly valued as a customer? Recreate that sentiment for your clientele. Celebrate milestones with them, whether it's their tenth visit or their first year as a customer. Offer an unexpected upgrade, a sample of a new strain, or a discount on their favorite product. These moments blossom into stories they share with friends, seeding potential new customers.

In the dance of dialogue, don't shy away from direct questions. Ask your customers what they desire, what they think of your products, and what they would change. This not only provides you with invaluable insights but also makes them feel involved, and part of the growth of your business. Remember, every word spoken, and every gesture made, contributes to the symphony of your service. A one-line thank you note with an order can resonate louder than the most elaborate marketing campaign. As you write your story in the pages of the cannabis industry, ensure it's one that's told and retold through the experiences of loyal customers who've become not just consumers but advocates, friends, and the most potent part of your success.

Lastly, amidst the green rush, simplicity is key. Don't cloud the air with complex programs or convoluted incentives. Clarity is the scent that lingers, the quality that brings customers back through your doors – time and time again. Listen to the rhythm of your business, the ebb and flow of customer needs, and adapt. Incorporate their words into your narrative. "I stay because here, I'm not just another sale; I'm part of a community," a devoted patron once shared. This testament should be the essence of your loyalty program.

In conclusion, show your customers their worth through every facet of your business, from the first welcoming smile to the personalized thank-you as they depart. In doing so, you'll not only grow a loyal customer base but also cultivate a thriving cannabis community that stands the test of time.

Product Launches and Promotions

As I mentioned earlier in the segment on branding, when you get ready to introduce a product and get it out to the public, brand association is crucial to jumpstarting a business. If you pay attention to a lot of the major brands across the United States, a lot of those brands are associated with celebrities, mainly hip-hop artists. One of the most successful and well-known brands in the industry is the Cookies brand. That brand is associated with hip-hop artist, Burner, who has been in the industry, a long time like myself. I've created a brand myself called Hip-Hop Legacy Brand and I have associated it with legendary artists in the hip-hop industry and it has served me well. I have several stores in Thailand that are literally called Hip-Hop Legacy Brands and we get tons of customers, based on the fact that cannabis and the hip-hop world seem to go hand-in- hand. So doing good promotions, having autograph sessions handing out swag, and attaching it to a musician, celebrity or athlete has paid off pretty well in this industry. That doesn't guarantee success, because if you choose the wrong artist or celebrity who doesn't have any affiliation with the cannabis industry their brands don't do so well. Like I've always said, cannabis is a culture and the culture recognizes whose fake and whose real. So be careful when you go out and grab influencers that are not of the industry - it can backfire. It's these little bits like this that can make you an average person or a million-dollar brand in the cannabis space!

NEW PRODUCT LAUNCH

In the ever-evolving tapestry of the cannabis industry, where the entrepreneurial spirit blazes as fiercely as the product itself, a pioneering business must not only grow but also glow amidst the competition. The art of unveiling new products and orchestrating promotional campaigns is a symphony that, when played right, can resonate across markets and consumer segments, leading to a crescendo of success and profitability.

Embarking on this journey, it is imperative to map out the strategic route we have taken to navigate the complex landscape of product launches and promotions. This blueprint is not just a path previously trodden but also a guide for burgeoning enterprises seeking to replicate our triumphs.

The pivotal points that we will unfold are:

1. Market Research and Consumer Insights

2. Developing a Compelling Value Proposition

3. Crafting a Memorable Brand Experience

4. Strategic Timing and Seasonal Tie-ins

5. Multi-Channel Marketing and Outreach

6. Post-Launch Analysis and Feedback

Before a single seed of a new product idea is planted, it is crucial to understand the soil – the market. Market research and consumer insights provide the fertile ground for your ideas to take root. By analyzing trends, understanding competitor strategies, and listening to the voice of the customer, one can identify gaps and opportunities that a new product might fill.

Detail Expansion

Dive deep into demographic studies, surveys, focus groups, and sales data. This research will illuminate the desires and pain points of your target audience. As we launched our pioneering cannabis-infused edibles, it was the voice of health-conscious consumers that guided our formulation – low-calorie, sugar-free options that were a resounding hit.

Evidence and Testimonials

Customer testimonials and market data are your best advocates. Upon release, our edibles were complemented by rave reviews from fitness enthusiasts who had long sought after healthier ways to enjoy cannabis. Sales figures mirrored this enthusiasm, with a significant uptick in a demographic previously untapped by our competitors.

Practical Applications

Use these insights to tailor your product development. If your research indicates a yearning for organic products, then let that be the seed from which your product grows. Engage with your audience early on, even before launch, to foster anticipation and validate your direction. Your product must not only exist; it must sing a sirens' song, luring customers with a promise that resonates with their deepest needs and desires.

Detail Expansion

A value proposition is the core of your product's identity. It's what sets it apart from the rest. For our line of vapes, we didn't just promise a high; we promised an adventure. Each flavor was crafted to evoke a journey – 'Alpine Bliss', 'Desert Sunset', 'Urban Rush' – and our customers bought not just a product but an experience.

Evidence and Testimonials

The response was visual and visceral. Customers shared pictures of their 'adventures,' tagging us in landscapes where they enjoyed our vapes. These authentic endorsements were more powerful than any ad campaign we could have commissioned.

Practical Applications

Craft your narrative around the value proposition. Every piece of marketing material, every social media post, and every package should echo this message. When customers see your product, they should think not just of what it is, but what it represents. In a sea of green, how do you make your leaf stand out? Through a brand experience that etches itself into the memory of your customers.

Detail Expansion

The brand experience extends beyond the product. It's the aroma that greets the customers as they enter your store, the texture of the packaging in their hands, and the tone of the conversation they have with your staff. For our dispensary, we designed an ambiance that spoke of sophistication and safety, aligning with our target market's preference for a high-end cannabis experience.

Evidence and Testimonials

Our clientele's feedback was overwhelmingly positive. They didn't just come to shop; they came for the atmosphere. The ambiance became a talking point, as much a part of our brand as the products on our shelves.

Practical Applications

Consider every touchpoint with your customer. From the design of your retail space to your online presence, ensure consistency and quality. This conveys a message to your customers: we care about your experience. A launch is not just about the 'what' but also the 'when'. Timing can be the difference between a fizzle and a fireworks show.

Detail Expansion

Aligning product launches with cultural events, seasons, or holidays can amplify your reach. Our 'Summer Solstice Sativa' was a hit because it was more than a strain; it was a celebration of the longest day of the year, a product that became part of the summer narrative.

Evidence and Testimonials

Sales data spiked around the solstice, and customer engagement on social media soared as they associated our product with their summer festivities.

Practical Applications

Plan your launch calendar with precision. Anticipate and leverage periods of high consumer engagement to maximize impact. If you're launching a relaxing indica strain, why not time it around National Relaxation Day? In today's digital age, your marketing must be omnipresent – a harmonious chorus heard across various platforms.

Detail Expansion

We leveraged a multi-channel approach, combining traditional media with digital platforms. Our campaigns ran on radio and in print, but also on Instagram and Twitter, reaching different demographics in spaces they frequented.

Evidence and Testimonials

Our analytics showed increased engagement rates from our social media ads, translating to higher web traffic and, ultimately, more sales.

Practical Applications

Craft your message to suit the medium. A tweet is not a press release; an Instagram post isn't a billboard. Tailor your content to fit the channel and the audience that inhabits it. The launch is just the beginning. The true measure of success is in the sustained flight that follows.

Detail Expansion

Post-launch analysis involves sifting through sales data, customer feedback, and market response. This is where you learn what soared and what sank. We poured over every detail after our launches, seeking insights to refine our future efforts.

Evidence and Testimonials

Our post-launch surveys revealed that while our products were well-received, there was a craving for more variety in our edible line. Acting on this, we expanded our offerings, which led to a significant increase in customer satisfaction and repeat purchases.

Practical Applications

Use the data to guide your next steps. Make adjustments based on what your customers tell you, and don't be afraid to pivot if necessary. The market is always speaking; make sure you're listening. As we weave through the intricacies of product launches and promotions, let us not forget the fluidity required to transition from one chapter to the next. The cannabis industry is a living, breathing entity that demands adaptability and finesse. Have you ever pondered the gravity of timing in your product launches? How often do you analyze the echoes of your market's needs? With each step, remember that you are not merely selling a product; you are curating an experience, crafting a story, and sowing the seeds for a bountiful harvest.

The cannabis industry is not just about the product; it's about the story you tell, the experience you provide, and the journey you offer. It's a saga of sensation, a narrative of novelty. In this grand story, your product launches and promotions are but chapters that enthrall and captivate, leaving your audience yearning for more.

CHAPTER FIVE

INVOLVING THE HEMP INDUSTRY: CBD AND THC CROSS OVER PRODUCTS

Delta 9 and Delta 8 Hemp Opportunities

One of the biggest roadblocks to being in the cannabis industry and running it like a regular business is course its Schedule One designation. So none of the regular business plans or traditional ways of running a business, whether financing, marketing, branding or simply finding a location, is easy. So what helped me in really getting my products across was when I became a member of the National Hemp Association. Shortly afterward, I became the chair of the Social Equity Standing Committee for the National Hemp Association. That gave me a big up in the cannabis space because I realized that cannabis and hemp are so similar and when the 2018 Farm Bill passed that allowed CBD products to be manufactured and sold throughout the country in the world. It was a game changer because the farm bill allowed for products like Delta Eight and other derivatives of hemp that also gave a psychoactive effect, which was an avenue that people used to get their products out there. This is a surefire way of branding yourself within the same market that you eventually want to sell your THC products to.

In the burgeoning landscape of the cannabis industry, a new era has dawned—one where Delta 9 and Delta 8 hemp not only represent burgeoning markets but also exemplify the remarkable potential of technology in transforming green gold into real gold. As we delve into the intricacies of these opportunities, let's unfold how you, the pioneering entrepreneur, can harness these innovations for monumental success.

Understanding the molecular dance of cannabinoids like Delta 9 and Delta 8 THC is akin to deciphering a secret language that unlocks vast potential. Delta 9 THC, the most well-known cannabinoid, is synonymous with the psychoactive properties of cannabis. Delta 8, its less potent cousin, offers a gentler high and is rapidly gaining popularity for its unique effects and legal status in many regions. Both have immense market potential, but how does one navigate these waters with the compass of technology?

Imagine a world where cultivation is not just an art but a precise science. Advanced LED lighting systems that mimic the sun's natural spectrum, hydroponic setups that deliver nutrients with surgical accuracy, and climate-controlled environments that can be adjusted with the tap of a screen—these are the tools of the modern cannabis cultivator. Such innovations not only increase yield and potency but also offer consistency, a trait highly valued in the pharmaceutical-grade cannabis market.

Take, for instance, the story of a Colorado-based startup that leveraged data analytics to optimize its growth cycle. By tracking every variable from humidity to soil pH and cross-referencing it with production output, they unlocked patterns that led to a 30% increase in Delta 9 THC concentration. What's more, by isolating Delta 8 THC during extraction, they opened a new product line that catered to consumers looking for a milder experience.

But what does this mean for you, the reader, who might be asking, "How can I turn these insights into a profitable enterprise?" It's about understanding the market demand and

aligning it with technological advancements. With the right equipment and know-how, small-scale operations can compete with industry giants, carving out a niche in specialized, high-quality products.

Consider the complexity of extraction techniques. Supercritical CO_2 extraction, once a method reserved for large-scale manufacturers, is now accessible to small business owners thanks to the advent of more affordable and user-friendly machines. This method preserves the integrity of cannabinoids and terpenes, ensuring a purer, more potent product—a selling point that can't be overstated in a marketplace that's becoming increasingly discerning.

But let's not overlook the importance of compliance and safety. As Delta 8 ventures into a legal gray area, the savvy entrepreneur must stay abreast of legislation. Utilizing blockchain for seed-to-sale tracking not only ensures transparency and builds trust with consumers, but it also positions your business as a responsible entity, ready to adapt to regulatory changes.

Data and facts form the backbone of any successful venture. Recent studies suggest that the Delta 8 market is projected to grow at an astounding rate, with some estimates placing its value at billions within the next five years. This is a segment ripe for innovation, where technology can be the differentiator between a product that's merely good and one that's truly exceptional.

Clarifying complex terms is essential in this niche. For instance, "isomerization" may sound daunting, but it's simply a process where CBD, which is abundant in hemp, is converted into Delta 9 THC or Delta 8 THC. Understanding this chemistry is crucial for product development and diversification.

Remember the key takeaways: Delta 9 and Delta 8 THC markets are fertile grounds for technological innovation; from cultivation to extraction, the integration of technology is essential for competitive advantage; and staying informed about legislation and consumer trends will guide your decisions in this dynamic industry. These markets allow you to brand your products in a federally legal space so you can take advantage of normal business practices.

A Quality Cannabis Supply Chain and Logistics

One thing that makes a cannabis business flourish with ease is having access to quality products. Therefore, having connections to other licenses within the cannabis, space is crucial to the success of your business. Except for micro businesses, of which usually have all their licenses in-house, it is very important to have, good relationships with your colleagues who hold other licenses within the cannabis space. I have had many instances where if I did not have a good relationship with my manufacturers or cultivators then when I ran out of product, I would have lost lots of money during that period.

Because people don't like being without, their cannabis products. Because there are so many other options, in some states that are already mature if you don't have what a person wants they will go right to the next store. Or if your main vendor is out and you don't have plans put in place they will seek to get their supplies from another manufacturer and the sequence goes on and on per type of licensee. One of the

processes that were put in for the social equity licenses was that each of the social equity licenses had to receive a certain percentage of their product from another social equity licensee that ensured that all of the licenses would have products for their businesses to flourish. I think this was an excellent idea to make sure that everyone has a fair shot. In the state of Illinois, where multi-state operators have a strong foothold on the market there, laws were put into place that forced them to purchase a certain amount of products from other people so that they couldn't monopolize the market because most of them are micro-businesses who are vertically integrated so they could undercut the market with their prices. Having good supply chains in the cannabis industry is of paramount importance for several reasons:

1. Quality Control: A well-managed supply chain ensures that high-quality cannabis products are consistently delivered to consumers. This includes maintaining the integrity of the product from cultivation through to retail.

2. Regulatory Compliance: The cannabis industry is heavily regulated, and a good supply chain helps ensure compliance with all laws and regulations at each stage, from seed-to-sale tracking to proper testing and distribution practices.

3. Efficiency and Cost Management: Efficient supply chains can reduce waste, lower costs, and improve profit margins. This is particularly important in the cannabis industry, where profit margins can be thin due to high regulatory costs and taxes.

4. Meeting Consumer Demand: A reliable supply chain is essential for meeting consumer demand promptly. This includes having the right products available when and where consumers want them.

5. Risk Management: Good supply chain management helps mitigate risks such as product shortages, delays, and quality issues. This is crucial in maintaining a good reputation and customer trust.

6. Adaptability: The cannabis industry is rapidly evolving, and supply chains must be adaptable to respond to changes in consumer preferences, market conditions, and regulations.

7. Scalability: As businesses grow, their supply chains must be able to scale up to meet increased production and distribution needs. A well-designed supply chain can facilitate this growth.

8. Innovation: A strong supply chain supports innovation by enabling

the introduction of new products and technologies into the market.

Amid the green rush, where pioneers and entrepreneurs race to stake their claims in the fertile plains of the cannabis industry, one critical factor often determines the victor from the vanquished: the supply chain. A seamless flow from seed to sale is the lifeblood of any cannabis enterprise, yet it remains one of the most complex and underestimated challenges in the industry.

As we delve into the labyrinth of logistics, let's illuminate the current landscape. The market is burgeoning, and demand is sky-high, yet many businesses find themselves entangled in a web of inefficiency, where the promise of profit is choked by the vines of disarray. The primary issue at hand is a supply chain fraught with fragmentation, opacity, and vulnerability to regulatory shifts that can alter the terrain overnight.

What, then, are the potential consequences if you don't have a solid supply chain and people you can trust? Picture this: crops of premium cannabis await shipment, but due to a lack of coordination, they miss their delivery windows, leading to a cascade of delays. Retail shelves stay barren, customers turn to competitors, and hard-earned reputations wilt. The ripple effects can be devastating—a single snag in the supply chain can unravel the fabric of an enterprise, leading to financial losses and squandered opportunities.

So, how does one navigate this tangled network? The solution lies in optimizing the supply chain for efficiency and reliability. This means implementing a robust logistics strategy, one that not only addresses current challenges but is also adaptable to the evolving landscape of cannabis distribution. Let's chart the course for this strategy. The first step is the integration of technology—specifically, seed-to-sale software that tracks the product journey with surgical precision. This digital ledger not only ensures regulatory compliance but also offers real-time data that can be used to streamline operations.

Next, we must build relationships with reliable transportation partners who understand the nuances of cannabis logistics. These alliances are crucial in ensuring that products move swiftly and safely to their destinations. To complement this, investing in quality packaging is a must—products need to be protected from degradation, preserving their potency and purity. But how does one ensure the solution's efficacy? Look no further than the pioneers like myself who've already blazed this trail. There are tales of businesses that have seen a dramatic reduction in waste, cost savings, and an uptick in customer satisfaction simply by adopting more sophisticated tracking systems. These are not merely anecdotes but beacons that guide the way forward. And what of alternative solutions? Some advocate for the vertical integration of supply chains, where control over every aspect from cultivation to retail is maintained in-house. While this approach has merits, such as increased control and potentially higher margins, it also requires significant capital and carries the risk of overextension.

The path to millions in the cannabis industry is paved with more than just good intentions or green thumbs. Remember, in this ever-expanding field, the most successful are not just growers or sellers, but those who can ensure that their bounty flows unfettered from farm to fingertips.

Branding THC Products Through the CBD Market

The burgeoning world of cannabis is a kaleidoscope of opportunity, with its colors most vivid in the branding and marketing of THC products. As pioneers in the industry, we've come to understand that the landscape is not just about cultivation or quality, but also about perception, recognition, and loyalty. This is where the legal CBD market comes into play, offering a unique avenue for THC cannabis brands to establish themselves and flourish.

Imagine, if you will, a world where THC products are as easily recognized and as widely accepted as any mainstream commodity. This vision is becoming increasingly tangible through the strategic utilization of the CBD market. CBD, known for its legal status and health benefits, serves as the perfect trojan horse for THC branding, setting the stage for consumer familiarity and trust.

The assertion here is clear: Branding THC products through the CBD market is not just advantageous but necessary for businesses aiming to make an indelible mark in the

cannabis industry. Let's explore this proposition further with concrete evidence.

Consider the case of a CBD brand that has successfully captivated the market. Their products are in high demand, their logo is instantly recognizable, and their customer loyalty is robust. Now, introduce their THC-infused line. The brand has already laid the groundwork for consumer confidence, which translates into a smoother introduction of THC products to the market. This is not mere speculation; market research indicates that consumers are more likely to try new products from brands they already know and trust.

Let's delve deeper into this evidence. Statistics from states with legalized cannabis show a significant overlap between CBD and THC consumers. People are using CBD for wellness and are open to exploring THC for similar or complementary uses. A survey reveals that over 60% of CBD users are inclined to purchase THC products from the same brand, highlighting the immense potential for cross-promotion and brand extension. However, it would be remiss not to acknowledge the counterarguments. Skeptics point out the differences in regulation between CBD and THC, suggesting that intertwining the two could lead to legal complications or consumer confusion. Indeed, THC's legal status remains a patchwork of state laws, whereas CBD derived from hemp enjoys a far broader legality under federal law.

Yet, this counter-evidence does not discount the initial claim but rather underscores the need for clarity and compliance in branding efforts. THC brands can navigate these regulatory waters by maintaining distinct product lines while leveraging the established reputation of their CBD counterparts. Furthermore, clear labeling and consumer education can effectively mitigate any potential confusion, turning this challenge into an opportunity for transparency and trust-building.

Additional supporting evidence comes from branding successes in other industries. For instance, consider the organic food market. Once niche and misunderstood, organic brands used their health-focused positioning to expand into other sectors of the grocery industry. Today, many of these brands have portfolios that span a variety of products, capitalizing on their established reputation within the organic market to introduce new items to their loyal customer base.

The journey to making millions in the cannabis industry is not just about the product but also about the story you weave and the trust you build. Branding THC products through the CBD market is a strategic move that harnesses legality, consumer perception, and market trends to create a formidable brand presence. It is an approach rooted in the understanding that, in this pioneering space, the brands that resonate with consumers on multiple levels will be the ones that endure and prosper. As you turn the pages of this book and chart your own course in the cannabis industry, consider the power of the CBD market not just as a companion to THC, but as a foundation upon which empires are built.

Hemp and CBD Market Expansion

As I stated earlier, I chair a committee with the National Hemp Association, one of America's premier and longest-running hemp organizations. What I have found is that the pathway to making millions in the cannabis industry is not the only way to take advantage of this wonderful plant historically known as " Cannabis Sativa ". The Hemp Industry, especially the industrial hemp industry has a long history in this country, as well as the world, and is making a comeback of its own. In the tapestry of American industry, few threads have woven as complex and colorful a pattern as that of cannabis. To truly grasp the significance of the hemp and CBD market expansion, we must cast our gaze back to the roots of prohibition.

Travel Back in Time

The year is 1937, and the United States Congress passed the Marihuana Tax Act, placing heavy taxes on the sale of cannabis, essentially marking the beginning of the prohibition era for the plant. From this point on, hemp, despite its lack of psychoactive properties, is grouped with marijuana and falls out of favor, and years of potential growth are stifled by regulatory restrictions.

Historical Milestones

Fast forward to the late 20th century, a whisper of change begins to rustle through the branches of legislation. The Controlled Substances Act of 1970 categorizes all forms of cannabis, including hemp, as a Schedule I drug, illegal under federal law. However, the turn of the millennium heralds a new era, with states like California pioneering the medicinal cannabis movement. Then, a monumental shift occurred in 2014 when the Farm Bill allowed for state-regulated hemp research programs.

From Past to Present

This legislative evolution sets the stage for the 2018 Farm Bill, which decouples hemp from marijuana, defining it as any part of the cannabis plant with less than 0.3% THC. This reclassification opens the floodgates for the hemp and

CBD industry, allowing for legal cultivation, production, and sale of these products, ushering in an era of unprecedented opportunity. Today, we stand at the crossroads of history and potential, the green fields of hemp stretching out before us, ripe with possibility.

Why History Matters Now

Understanding this history is not merely an academic pursuit; it is crucial for grasping the complexities of today's market and recognizing the volatility and the potential that comes with a once-forbidden industry now stepping into the light. The past teaches us not just about the battles fought and won but also about the resilience of an industry that has much to offer in terms of health, sustainability, and economic growth.

Segue to the Story

As we pivot from the historical canvas to today's vibrant market, let's delve into the heart of the modern hemp and CBD expansion. What does this mean for entrepreneurs, consumers, and the future of American industry?

The landscape of legal hemp cultivation has transformed the face of agriculture, with acres dedicated to this versatile crop stretching across states that once could not imagine such a turn of events. The CBD market, a gem in the crown of hemp's offerings, is projected to reach astronomical figures, with experts estimating billions in sales within the next few years. Have you ever stopped to consider the boundless potential that lies within a single hemp seed? This tiny vessel carries not just the blueprint for a plant but also for an entire industry. The fibers can create textiles that rival any synthetic counterpart, the seeds can nourish with their rich oil, and the extracted CBD has opened a world of wellness and therapeutic promise.

Yet, the road to riches in this green revolution is not a straight path. It winds and turns, with legal intricacies and market fluctuations acting as both obstacles and catalysts. How then can one navigate this labyrinth to emerge victorious? The answer lies in a confluence of savvy entrepreneurship, consumer education, and legislative advocacy. To thrive in the hemp and CBD market, one must be as dynamic as the industry itself, adapting to legal changes, consumer trends, and technological advancements.

Let us not forget the power of perception. Hemp's image has undergone a remarkable metamorphosis, from a misunderstood cousin of marijuana to a symbol of health and sustainability. This rebranding is not accidental but the result of concerted efforts by those within the industry to reshape public opinion. What sets apart the successful players in this green rush is their ability to tell a compelling story, to forge a connection with the consumer that transcends the product itself. It is about creating an experience, a lifestyle, and a community.

Chapter Six

THE PEOPLE'S PLANT: SOCIAL EQUITY AND ADVOCACY

The Role of Cannabis in Social Justice

As an African American pioneer in this industry, and literally being one of, if not the first African American to have a legal cannabis business in the United States, I have personal experience with the need for social equity within the cannabis space. When I first started out on this journey, I opened one of what was later to be named a Dispensary, but at that time was simply known as a collective based on the laws in California, I figured that this would be an industry that people who looked like me would flourish in. This was of course based on America's history, and what many people had to do to survive from my socioeconomic background. I was also very happy and confident as we begin to move the needle on medical marijuana acceptance across the United States, that there would finally be an industry in which minorities and women, especially Black people would have an advantage. This was based on our association with cannabis, and the actual number of African Americans who were sentenced to jail or prison, based on cannabis-related offenses over our white counterparts. Well to my disappointment, as cannabis became more and more accepted because of the actual work done by people like myself, whether it be from documentaries that I participated in or magazine articles that I have been written about in over a decade or so I figured that once things became more legal we would have a leg up in this industry. Unfortunately, because these were real businesses, and with the lack of banking, along with the rules and regulations were written by people who did not look like me there still were things put in place that kept minorities from being awarded these licenses. When the data was collected after states like California, Colorado, Washington, and Oregon became legal, it was abundantly clear that over 90% of the licenses that were given out were given out to white males in this country. So of course, guys like myself, who had literally fought on the front lines along with my colleagues that are in jail, who had been put in jail and gone through all types of havoc. I was not going to stand idly by and not see minorities not being able to participate in this industry, for whatever reason or excuse that was given to us. So during that time, we came up with the terminology and idea of social equity here in California to address the disparity in licenses given out in this country. We were some of the first ones to get legislation passed and get our elected officials to promote the social equity program.

The social equity program across the United States, then made it a priority to give licenses to people whose lives and/or neighborhoods were affected by the failed war on drugs. This was usually in black and brown neighborhoods so because of that, a certain amount of licenses were allocated to people from those neighborhoods which helped to change the ratio of licenses given out to minorities in this country. Because of the lack of banking and investors within this industry, with all of the social equity licenses that have been given out, there is an opportunity for investors to team up with these individuals to participate in the cannabis industry. I would strongly advise anyone who is looking to get into the industry to reach out to and find out about the social equity programs within your state. This may be one of the easiest ways to get into the industry because a lot of the work would have already been done by the social equity license awardee.

The role of cannabis in social justice is multifaceted and has been increasingly recognized in recent years. The legalization and regulation of cannabis have been seen

as opportunities to address social inequities, particularly those related to racial disparities in drug enforcement. Historically, cannabis prohibition has dispro-portionately affected disadvantaged minority populations, with people of color being significantly more likely to be arrested for cannabis-related offenses. This has led to calls for cannabis reform to include social justice measures, such as expungement of previous arrests and convictions for cannabis-related crimes, and the implementation of social equity programs. Social equity programs aim to ensure that those most affected by cannabis prohibition, including people of color and those with prior marijuana offenses, are given opportunities to participate in the burgeoning cannabis industry. These programs can include measures such as prioritizing licensing for minority-owned businesses, provid-ing financial assistance or resources for those entering the industry, and reinvest-ing cannabis tax revenue into communities most affected by prohibition. States like Illinois, New York, New Jersey, and others have recognized the importance of going beyond expungement and have implemented comprehensive social equity programs. These programs aim to address the economic, educational, and wealth-building opportunities missed due to cannabis convictions. For instance, New York's Marijuana Regulation and Taxation Act focuses on racial and social justice, aiming to create equity-building and community reinvestment opportunities. However, the implementation of social equity in cannabis legislation has its challenges. Some critics argue that the commercialization of cannabis exacerbates many of the issues it aims to address, such as incarceration and reformation. Others point out that the transition from illicit to legal cannabis has not always resulted in social justice, with concerns about the diversity of the cannabis industry and the potential for cannabis legalization to negatively impact the populations that most suffered under prohibition. In conclusion. The role of cannabis in social justice is a complex and evolving issue. While cannabis reform presents opportunities to address historical social inequities, it also presents challenges that require careful consideration and ongoing evaluation. The ultimate goal is to create a diverse, equitable, and inclusive cannabis industry that rectifies the social and economic harms of prohibition

To ensure that social equity programs are effectively implemented in the cannabis industry, addressing the main challenges of access to capital and financing, licensing and regulatory barriers, and program evaluation and accountability is essential. Here are some strategies to tackle these challenges:

1. Access to Capital and Financing

2. Partnerships with Private Investors: Encourage partnerships with private investors, including venture capital funds and angel investors, who are interested in supporting social equity initiatives

3. Government Grants and Loans: Advocate for government grants and loans specifically designed to support social equity applicants in the cannabis industry

4. Community Development Financial Institutions (CDFIs): Work with CDFIs that provide financial services to underserved communities and can offer loans and financial assistance to social equity applicants.

5. Licensing and Regulatory Barriers

6. Streamlined Application Processes: Simplify the licensing application process for social equity applicants, potentially by reducing paperwork and providing clear guidelines

7. Technical Assistance: Offer technical assistance programs to help social equity applicants

8. navigate the complex regulatory environment and successfully apply for licenses

9. Policy Advocacy: Engage in policy advocacy to influence the creation of more inclusive and equitable licensing regulations that lower barriers for entry

10. Program Evaluation and Accountability

11. Transparent Metrics: Establish clear and transparent metrics to measure the success of social equity programs and ensure that they are meeting their intended goals

12. Regular Reporting: Implement regular reporting requirements for social equity programs to track progress and identify areas for improvement

13. Community Involvement: Involve community stakeholders in the evaluation process to ensure that social equity programs are accountable to the communities they are designed to serve

14. By focusing on these strategies, the cannabis industry can work to-

wards more effective implementation of social equity programs, ensuring that they provide meaningful opportunities for communities of color and those disproportionately affected by cannabis prohibition. It's also important to continuously review and adapt these strategies as the industry evolves and new insights are gained from the implementation of social equity programs in various jurisdictions

Participating in Social Equity Programs

Embarking on the journey to make your mark in the cannabis industry can be a transformative endeavor, especially when you align your pursuits with the noble cause of social equity. The goal? To not only thrive in this burgeoning sector but also to give back, ensuring that the economic benefits of cannabis legalization are shared inclusively. It's an opportunity to become an integral part of a movement that rectifies past injustices while building a sustainable future.

To set sail on this venture, you'll need a compass of prerequisites: a clear understanding of social equity programs, eligibility criteria, a business plan attuned to these initiatives, and perhaps most importantly, a steadfast commitment to the ethos of social justice. Let's dive into the detailed steps. Your first port of call is research. Ground yourself in the history of cannabis prohibition and its disproportionate impact on marginalized communities. Understand the legislation that has been passed to address these disparities. Different states have different guidelines and definitions of what constitutes a social equity applicant. Are you a resident of an area disproportionately affected by previous cannabis laws? Do you or your family members have a history of cannabis-related offenses? These are the types of questions that will define your path.

Next, fortify your vessel with knowledge. Attend workshops, webinars, and community meetings to immerse yourself in the culture and language of cannabis equity. Forge alliances with like-minded entrepreneurs and social advocates who share your vision. Their insights can be as valuable as a lighthouse guiding ships in the night. Now, you're ready to craft a business plan that is both profitable and progressive. Detail how your business will contribute to the goals of social equity. Will you provide employment opportunities to those hardest hit by cannabis criminalization? Perhaps you'll offer mentorship or educational programs. Here, your mission is twofold: to generate wealth and to uplift others. As you chart this course, heed the advice of those who have navigated these waters before you. One seasoned captain in the industry once said, "Social equity isn't a sprint; it's a marathon with hurdles." Patience and perseverance will be your closest allies.

The journey to making millions in the cannabis industry while participating in social equity programs is one filled with potential pitfalls and high peaks. It requires a navigator who is astute, socially conscious, and unerringly optimistic. The endeavor is not merely about personal gain but about sowing seeds of change that will flourish long after you've reaped your harvest.

Are you ready to take this path less traveled? It's a route that demands more than just business acumen; it calls for a heart aligned with justice and equity. If you find yourself nodding along, then perhaps you are the pioneer this industry needs—a beacon of progress in the green revolution. In the end, the story you'll tell won't just be one of financial success. It will be a narrative of transformation, of barriers broken, and of a community uplifted. This is more than a business venture; it's a legacy in the making.

Participating in social equity programs in the cannabis industry involves understanding the eligibility criteria, application process, and benefits offered by these programs. Here's a detailed guide on how to participate:

Eligibility Criteria

Eligibility for social equity programs often depends on factors such as residency, income, and previous cannabis convictions. For instance, in Illinois, a social equity applicant must have at least 51% ownership and control by one or more individuals who have lived in a Disproportionately Impacted Area for 5 of the past 10 years, have been arrested for or convicted of cannabis-related offenses eligible for expungement, or have more than 10 full-time employees, half of whom meet the aforementioned criteria

Application Process

The application process varies by state and program. For example, the Massachusetts Social Equity Program offers a free, statewide technical assistance and training program that creates sustainable pathways into the cannabis industry. Interested individuals can apply online when the application window opens. Similarly, the Illinois Cannabis Social Equity Program provides low-interest forgivable loans, legal assistance, technical assistance, and individualized support to social equity licensees

Benefits

Social equity programs offer a range of benefits to participants. These can include access to capital and financing, technical support, priority application processing, and reduced or waived fees. In Illinois, qualified social equity applicants are given a 50%

discount on all application fees, licensing fees, and other financial requirements. Some programs, like the Flowhub Social Equity Program, offer additional benefits such as discounted software for cannabis businesses.

1. Social equity applicants in the cannabis industry face a range of common challenges that can hinder their success and ability to compete with more established businesses. Here are some of the most prevalent issues:

2. Limited Access to Capital: One of the most significant barriers for social equity applicants is the difficulty in securing financing. Traditional banking services are often unavailable to cannabis businesses due to

federal restrictions, making it hard for these applicants to obtain loans and other financial services

3. Complicated Application Processes: The process of applying for a cannabis license can be complex and daunting, with a multitude of forms, fees, and legal requirements. This can be particularly challenging for those without prior experience in the cannabis industry or those without the resources to hire professional assistance

4.

5. Real Estate Challenges: Finding and securing suitable real estate for cannabis operations can be difficult and expensive. Social equity applicants often face real estate prices that are well above market rates, partly due to the limited number of properties that meet the zoning and regulatory requirements for cannabis businesses

6. Bureaucratic Logjams: Delays in the permitting process and other bureaucratic hurdles can stall the opening of a cannabis business. These delays can be costly and may result in the loss of property or other opportunities

7. Lack of Resources: Social equity applicants may lack the resources needed to navigate the cannabis industry successfully. This includes access to legal advice, business planning, and other professional services that are essential for establishing and running a cannabis business

8. Regulatory Challenges: The cannabis industry is heavily regulated, and staying compliant with all the laws and regulations can be a significant challenge, especially for new entrants who may not be familiar with the intricacies of cannabis legislation

9. Market Saturation: In some areas, the market may be saturated with cannabis businesses, making it difficult for new entrants, including social equity applicants, to gain a foothold and become profitable

10. Lack of Training: Social equity applicants may not have access to the same level of training and education as other entrepreneurs in the cannabis industry, which can put them at a disadvantage

11. Addressing these challenges is crucial for the success of social equity programs and for ensuring that the benefits of cannabis legalization are shared equitably. This may involve providing targeted support and resources to social equity applicants, simplifying the application process, and ensuring that these programs are adequately funded and managed.

Advocacy and Policy Influence

Being an advocate of social equity within the cannabis, space is one of the quickest ways to have a real impact as well as make millions within the industry. A lot of the time because of the disproportionate distribution of cannabis licenses throughout the United States minorities are being given a leg up to balance out the disproportionate distribution of cannabis licenses between white males and other minorities and women within this industry. This allows for a limited window, but a very important window for social equity businesses to open up without fear of competing with the large capital MSOs or as we

call them multi-state operators within the country. By having the market all to yourself for a year or two is a big deal because it allows you to establish your brand and establish contacts with your fellow social equity partners to already have a major foothold in your state or local jurisdiction before the big guys come onto the scene. This advantage can be the difference between being a regular guy or a multi-million dollar business within the cannabis world. But this all starts with advocacy and making sure you try to influence policy within your area so that you can get a social equity program going in your state. I did this in the city of Los Angeles and that work paved the way for many other states to follow. The cannabis industry had come a long way, but the journey toward equitable policy and legislation was far from over. This is the story of how advocacy and true grit can shape the future, and how I, Calvin Frye, played my part in this historic transformation.

The scene was set against the backdrop of a society in flux. Cannabis, once demonized and prohibited, was gradually being recognized for its medical benefits and economic potential. Yet, the shackles of outdated laws remained, a barrier to progress that needed dismantling. The main players in this narrative were a coalition of activists, business leaders, and legislators—the pioneers of a new age, determined to forge a path that others could follow.

Our core challenge was clear: to influence policy and advocate for the cannabis industry in a landscape riddled with stigma and resistance. The mission was to create a legal framework that would not only allow the industry to thrive but also rectify the wrongs caused by the War on Drugs, which had disproportionately impacted minority communities.

The approach we took was multifaceted. As a seasoned activist and entrepreneur, I leveraged my experience to bridge the gap between the cannabis community and policymakers. We initiated grassroots campaigns, rallied support through social media, and held educational forums to enlighten the public and lawmakers about the benefits of cannabis legalization.

But the real work occurred behind the scenes, in the halls of power where decisions were made. We crafted compelling arguments backed by scientific research and economic data, demonstrating the potential for job creation, tax revenue, and medical advancements. We lobbied tirelessly, building relationships with key stakeholders and aligning ourselves with the broader movement for social justice.

The results were profound. Slowly, legislation began to shift. States across the country started to legalize cannabis, either for medical or recreational use, and the economic impact was immediate and significant. Jobs were created, tax revenue soared, and, most importantly, the gears began to turn on social equity programs designed to offer reparations to those most harmed by cannabis criminalization.

Yet, as I analyze and reflect upon those heady days, I recognize that our work was far from perfect. Criticisms arose that not enough was being done to ensure the promised social equity. Some accused us of being too focused on economic gains. It was a sobering reminder that the struggle for justice is ongoing, and that advocacy must never become complacency.

Visual aids such as infographics depicting the economic growth and the decrease in

incarceration rates for cannabis-related offenses provided a stark representation of the change we were enacting. But beyond the numbers, the real stories lay in the lives transformed by these policies—lives once blighted by unjust laws now given a chance to flourish.

This case study is but one thread in the larger tapestry of the cannabis industry's narrative. It speaks to the power of advocacy and the necessity of policy influence in shaping a fair and prosperous market. It underscores the importance of being an active participant in the democratic process, of lending one's voice to the chorus clamoring for change.

But where does one go from here? How does one ensure that the victories of today are not the complacencies of tomorrow? These are the questions that must linger in the minds of those who dare to call themselves pioneers.

CHAPTER SEVEN

THE GLOBAL GREEN OPPORTUNITY: INTERNATIONAL MARKETS AND EXPANSION

The International Legal Patchwork

As the early morning sun filters through a canopy of emerald leaves, a farmer in the verdant fields of Uruguay tends to his cannabis plants, each one swaying gently in the breeze. Half a world away, in the bustling streets of Amsterdam, a business owner unlocks the doors to his coffee shop, readying the space for the day's influx of patrons eager for a taste of legal cannabis. Deep in the South Pacific a dispensary owner happily opens its doors in Phuket Thailand. Meanwhile, in the United States, entrepreneurs navigate a complex maze of state laws and federal restrictions, each trying to carve out a piece of the burgeoning cannabis market.

These scenes illustrate the diverse legal landscapes that shape the global cannabis industry—a patchwork of regulations that can either cultivate opportunity or smother potential. In this chapter, we'll weave through the intricate tapestry of international cannabis laws, examining their similarities, differences, and the profound implications they bear on business. Why, one might ask, should we juxtapose the cannabis legislation of various countries? The answer lies in the rich insights such a comparison can yield for investors, entrepreneurs, and policymakers. By understanding the dynamics at play in different regions, one can identify emerging markets, anticipate shifts in consumer behavior, and influence legislative developments.

Our criteria for comparison are straightforward yet comprehensive. We'll assess the legal status of cannabis—whether it's prohibited, decriminalized, or legal for medical or recreational use. We'll also consider the regulatory frameworks governing production, distribution, and sales, as well as the cultural attitudes that underpin these laws. Uruguay and Canada stand as heralds of full legalization, with both nations having taken the bold step to fully regulate the cannabis market. In Uruguay, residents can grow up to six plants at home or join cannabis clubs, which cultivate plants for their members.

Canada's approach is more commercial, with licensed producers supplying a nationwide market that includes both brick-and-mortar dispensaries and online sales. These countries share the common vision of stripping away the stigma of cannabis, treating it instead as a commodity to be regulated akin to alcohol or tobacco. Yet, their regulatory frameworks differ. Canada imposes strict quality control and marketing restrictions, while Uruguay mandates that sales can only occur through pharmacies, limiting the commercial potential.

Contrast this with the United States, where the federal government maintains cannabis as an illegal substance, yet individual states assert their sovereignty. In states like Colorado and California, cannabis entrepreneurs flourish under state protection, creating a patchwork within the patchwork, where interstate commerce remains a distant dream. Visual aids, such as comparative charts and maps, can starkly highlight these differences, illustrating the kaleidoscope of legislation from country to country, state to state. From these comparisons, we glean that the path toward legalization is not linear but rather a complex interplay of societal values, economic considerations, and political will. Countries that have legalized cannabis grapple with international treaties and trade agreements, while those in prohibition navigate the pressures of a global shift toward liberalization.

The real-world relevance of this analysis cannot be overstated. In Europe, Germany's consideration of legalization could trigger a domino effect, encouraging neighboring countries to follow suit. In Africa, Lesotho's move to license cannabis cultivation for export has set the stage for the continent's entry into the global cannabis market. One must pause to wonder: what does this mean for the future of cannabis businesses? Will a global consensus on cannabis policy emerge, or will the disparities persist, creating niches for savvy entrepreneurs to exploit? This discourse is not merely academic; it carries significant weight for anyone involved in or considering entry into the cannabis market. As we stride further into this uncharted territory, the lessons drawn from our international counterparts will become beacons, guiding us through the haze of uncertainty.

Amid this legal labyrinth, one truth remains—cannabis has transcended its illicit roots to become a legitimate, profitable industry. As pioneers in this space, we have the unique opportunity to shape its trajectory, ensuring that as the industry grows, it does so with integrity and responsibility. In the end, the global cannabis industry is much like the plants themselves—rooted in local conditions, yet reaching for the sun, aspiring to heights that once seemed unattainable. The question then becomes, how high can this industry soar, and who will have the vision to lead it there?

Strategies for Global Expansion

Pioneering the industry here in the United States since 2005, I have always had my eye on global expansion. Ever since I starred in the documentary or shall I call it a "pot-a- mentary" called " Super High Me ", I have been at the forefront of the cannabis industry.

Over the years, I have appeared on many reality shows like " Storage Wars "'and other episodes on smaller networks like "Mary Mary". I've been written up in many magazines, and I have keynoted many of the major trade shows. What I noticed was the number of foreigners who were attending the shows and coming up to me afterward handing me out business cards and begging me to reach out to them to help them write rules and cannabis laws within their country. I went ahead and made the big leap once Thailand changed its laws to allow for medical and recreational use of cannabis in its country. I reached out to one of my friends who happened to be living in Thailand now, he is an ex- MMA fighter, and Hollywood actor who has appeared in many movies. He was very big in Japan before he moved to Thailand, and he kept me on top of all of the legislation in law before Thailand came on board. I eventually flew there and met with him and was introduced to some of the residents there that were already trying to get into the industry, but didn't have the expertise.

I worked out a deal with them and I have several dispensaries that I partnered with that go under my product brand Hip-Hop Legacy Brand. I am working with growers in northern Thailand to produce quality products to be distributed in my store in southern Thailand. I have been introduced to members of Parliament and I have appointments set up to meet with the Minister of Health to hopefully help them write rules and regulations for their medical marijuana programs that they want to introduce to the people of the country. The reality is as dawn breaks and the world awakes to the aroma of opportunity, the cannabis industry stands at the precipice of a new era. Beyond the amber waves of grain in North America and the golden coasts of Uruguay, lies a vast, untapped potential: the international cannabis market. The pioneers who first planted the seeds of this burgeoning industry in the United States knew the day would come when the green shoots of their labor would need to spread their leaves globally. That day is upon us.

The burgeoning international cannabis market whispers promises of prosperity, but it also murmurs warnings of complexity and risk. This landscape is fraught with legal intricacies, cultural nuances, and political sensitivities. To navigate these waters successfully, businesses must be equipped with a compass of knowledge and a map of strategy. The primary challenge lies in the stark differences in legislation and public perception from one country to the next. While some nations embrace the medical and economic benefits of cannabis, others hold fast to longstanding prohibitions. The consequences of ignoring these disparities are dire—failing to adapt to local markets can lead to financial loss, legal repercussions, and a tarnished reputation.

The solution to this quandary is a meticulous, well-informed approach to global expansion. It begins with rigorous research: understanding the legal, economic, and cultural environments of potential markets. This knowledge forms the bedrock upon which all strategies are built.

Implementation of this strategy demands a multi-faceted approach. It involves establishing local partnerships to navigate the intricacies of foreign regulations, tailoring products and marketing to align with cultural expectations, and lobbying for favorable legal changes. Patience is a virtue in this process, as is resilience. Entering a new market is akin to planting a new crop—it requires careful cultivation and time to grow. Evidence of this approach's efficacy is not merely anecdotal; it is etched in the success stories of those who have walked this path. Canadian companies, for instance, have made significant inroads into European markets by leveraging their experience in a regulated domestic market to gain credibility abroad. Their success underlines the importance of a reputation for quality and compliance in gaining a foothold in new territories.

But what of alternative solutions? Diversification is one such strategy, spreading risk across various markets to mitigate the impact of turbulence in any single region. Another is a focus on ancillary services—such as technology, consulting, and equipment—over direct cannabis sales, which may face fewer legal barriers. Let us delve deeper into the practical steps of global expansion. The first port of call is market analysis. Which nations show signs of softening their stance on cannabis? Where is the demand for medical cannabis surging? Is there a burgeoning culture of cannabis acceptance that might herald a shift in recreational laws?

Following this analysis, the next step is to engage with local experts—lawyers, cultural advisors, and business consultants—who can provide invaluable insights and guidance. Their expertise can illuminate the path forward and help sidestep potential pitfalls.

Then comes the establishment of local alliances. Finding the right partner—a local business with established distribution networks and a deep understanding of the market—is akin to finding a lighthouse in a storm. It is a beacon that can guide you safely to shore.

Do you see it? Can you envision the mosaic of global markets, each with its unique hue and pattern, coming together to form a tapestry of opportunity? It requires a visionary to recognize the pattern, a strategist to piece it together, and a pioneer like me to bring it to life. Dialogues with international partners will weave through the narrative, adding depth and authenticity to the tale of expansion. As we stand on the cusp of this global adventure, let us not forget the simplicity of our core mission—to bring healing, joy, and prosperity through the responsible cultivation and distribution of cannabis. We must never lose sight of the plant itself, the very root of our industry, which demands our respect and stewardship.

The story of global expansion in the cannabis industry is not just a narrative of profits and market shares—it is a saga of human endeavor. It is the tale of pioneers, like me, who dared to dream big, to reach out across borders and cultures, to unite the world under the banner of green leaves. How far will you go, and what stories will you tell when the smoke clears and your dreams take root in foreign soil? The answer lies within your grasp, and the time to act is now.

Import/Export and Global Supply Chains

In the labyrinthine world of international trade, the cannabis industry stands unique, its tendrils reaching into the furthest corners of the globe, its potential as vast as it is complex. The goal here is clear: to skillfully navigate the maze of global supply chains and import/export regulations, ensuring that your cannabis business thrives in the international arena. But how does one transform this goal into reality?

To begin this journey, one must first gather the necessary materials and prerequisites: a keen understanding of international laws and compliance; solid relationships with growers, manufacturers, and distributors; and an unshakable commitment to quality and security. A network of legal advisors, customs brokers, and logistics experts will be your guiding stars.

Now, picture the broad strokes of this undertaking: sourcing premium product, forging international partnerships, managing logistics, and staying compliant with a patchwork of laws. Each phase presents its own challenges and opportunities, and we shall traverse them all. Let's venture deeper, into the heart of the matter, and examine each step with the precision of a master artisan.

Sourcing your product requires diligence. It's not merely about finding the best cannabis; it's about finding the right partners who align with your values and vision. Are they sustainable? Do they adhere to the highest cultivation standards? When you're confident in your source, you've laid a solid foundation. Building international partnerships is akin to a delicate dance. It's about mutual respect, shared goals, and the subtle art of negotiation. When you find a partner whose rhythm matches yours, the possibilities are endless.

Managing logistics is perhaps the most intricate piece of the puzzle. It involves synchronizing countless moving parts—shipping schedules, customs clearance, quality control, and so much more. It's a task that demands precision and attention to detail. Staying compliant is not a one-time task but a continuous journey. Laws change; staying informed is imperative. Compliance is your shield against the slings and arrows of international trade. Now, let me offer you some nuggets of wisdom, gleaned from the trenches of experience. Always vet your partners thoroughly. An ounce of prevention is worth a pound of cure. Be vigilant about quality control; your reputation hinges on it. And never underestimate the importance of cultural understanding; it can make or break a deal. I can't emphasize doing your due diligence enough when choosing a foreign partner because there can be major implications if they are a "bad fruit"!

How does one know their efforts are bearing fruit? Testing or validation comes in various forms—successful shipments, satisfied partners, and the ultimate indicator: profit. Yet, it's also in the feedback from the end-users, the patients, and the customers whose lives you're touching. Their satisfaction is the truest measure of success. Troubleshooting is an inevitable part of this process. A shipment gets delayed at customs, a supplier encounters a crop failure, or a law changes overnight—these are but a few of the hurdles you might face. The key is to remain adaptable, and resourceful, and always have a contingency plan. Imagine, for a moment, the rich, earthy scent of cannabis as it's carefully packed for its journey across the sea. Picture the meticulous hands that tend to it, the sharp minds that navigate its course. Can you see the tapestry of global trade routes, each strand an essential lifeline to your business?

As you ponder this, remember that the world of cannabis is ever-evolving. What was true yesterday may not hold tomorrow. Ask yourself, are you prepared to adapt? To innovate? Do you have the courage to stand at the helm, steering your business through the tempest of international trade? By now, the image should be clear—the cannabis industry is not for the faint of heart. It demands a pioneer's spirit, a strategist's mind, and a poet's soul. It calls for leaders who can see beyond the horizon, and who understand that every seed planted, every shipment sent, and every law navigated is a step toward a greener future.

The path to making millions in the cannabis industry is paved with more than just good intentions; it's constructed with the bricks of knowledge, strategy, and relentless execution.

Partnerships and Global Networking

In the burgeoning world of the cannabis industry, the successful entrepreneur is akin to a masterful weaver, intertwining the threads of partnerships and global networking to create a resilient and profitable tapestry. The significance of cultivating robust relationships and expansive networks cannot be overstated, especially when these bonds transcend local markets and stretch across borders to stitch together a global community.

Before we delve into the particulars, let's acknowledge the profound impact that well- crafted partnerships and strategic networking have on a cannabis business's growth and scalability. These relationships are not merely accessories to your business model; they are the engine that drives innovation, expansion, and financial success.

1. Identifying Synergistic Partners

2. Leveraging International Trade Shows and Conferences

3. Cultivating Government and Regulatory Relationships

4. Maximizing Digital Platforms for Networking

5. Engaging in Cross-Cultural Exchange

Identifying Synergistic Partners*

The quest for the right business partners is compared to finding a kindred spirit in a crowd. It requires discernment, intuition, and a clear understanding of your own business's goals and values. Synergistic partners are those whose services, products, or missions align with your own, creating a symbiotic relationship where 1 + 1 equals far more than 2. Consider the story of Green Horizons, a cannabis start-up that partnered with an innovative packaging company. This partnership not only improved their product's shelf life but also elevated their brand image through sustainable and eye-catching designs.

In your venture, seek out partners who share your commitment to quality, sustainability, or whatever your core values might be. Look for those who can add value to your business, whether through technological expertise, market access, or brand enhancement.

Leveraging International Trade Shows and Conferences*

Trade shows and conferences are the fertile grounds where seeds of opportunity are sown. They provide a platform for entrepreneurs to showcase their offerings, learn about industry trends, and connect with potential partners, investors, and customers from around the globe. At the Cannabiz World Summit, numerous entrepreneurs have testified to striking deals that catapulted their local businesses into the international arena, all because they were present and engaged. Attend these gatherings with a strategy. Research attendees in advance, schedule meetings, and prepare to present your business compellingly. Post-event, follow up promptly to cement the connections you've made.

Cultivating Government and Regulatory Relationships*

Navigating the complex web of cannabis regulations requires allies in governmental and regulatory bodies. Establishing rapport with these stakeholders can provide insights into policy changes, streamline licensing processes, and offer a degree of protection against regulatory headwinds. A CEO of a flourishing cannabis enterprise once said, "Our early efforts to engage with regulators turned compliance from a hurdle into a competitive advantage."

Attend public hearings, participate in industry panels, and make your business's voice heard. Seek opportunities to collaborate on pilot programs or educational initiatives that can demonstrate your commitment to compliance and public safety.

Maximizing Digital Platforms for Networking*

In an age where digital presence is as substantial as physical presence, harnessing the power of online platforms for networking is indispensable. Social media, professional forums, and online marketplaces can connect you with peers, influencers, and thought leaders in the cannabis space. A cultivator from Colorado expanded his reach by connecting with international buyers through a well-respected online cannabis marketplace, thus opening up new revenue streams. Create engaging content, participate in relevant discussions, and use these platforms to showcase your expertise. Remember, the digital world knows no borders; your next strategic partner might be a click away.

Engaging in Cross-Cultural Exchange*

The cannabis industry is as culturally diverse as it is geographically expansive. Engaging in cross-cultural exchanges can lead to a deeper understanding of international markets, allowing for more effective and respectful business practices. A dispensary owner shared how learning about the cultural significance of cannabis in various countries helped tailor her product line to cater to an international clientele. Participate in cultural events, learn languages, and immerse yourself in the customs of the regions you wish to do business with. This not only aids in building rapport but also informs product development and marketing strategies.

As we segue from the potential of partnerships to the intricacies of networking, consider the depth of the ocean that is the global cannabis market. Are you ready to dive in, swim with the currents of international commerce, and emerge with treasures untold?

Think about it—when was the last time you reached beyond your comfort zone to shake hands with opportunity? What alliances await in the vast network of the global cannabis trade?

In the world of cannabis, as in life, your network is your net worth. Nurture it with care, and watch as the seeds you plant today bloom into the millions you aspire to make tomorrow. Facts homie!

CHAPTER EIGHT

INSIDER TIPS ON MAKING MILLIONS IN THE CANNABIS INDUSTRY

Its Not What You Know Its Who You Know.

I n the sprawling, verdant fields of opportunity that define the cannabis industry, there's a mantra whispered like a sacred incantation among those who've risen to the top: "It's not what you know, it's who you know." This maxim, as ancient as commerce itself, rings especially true in a sector where legal landscapes shift like dunes under a desert sun and where the green rush has attracted pioneers and prospectors alike.

At the heart of this burgeoning empire of green lies a simple truth: relationships are the lifeblood of business success. Having a robust network of industry leaders, established brand owners, and influencers can be the difference between a burgeoning enterprise and one that withers on the vine.

So, what's the cornerstone of this claim? Put simply, the cannabis industry, much like any other, operates on the currency of trust and mutual benefit. For those who've navigated the labyrinthine regulations and emerged victorious, their insights are invaluable. They've built bridges where others saw barriers, and their endorsements can catapult a new player into the limelight.

Consider, for instance, the story of Jane Doe, who leveraged her connections with seasoned dispensary owners to secure prime shelf space for her innovative edibles. The result? A surge in demand that outstripped supply, is a testament to the power of strategic alliances.

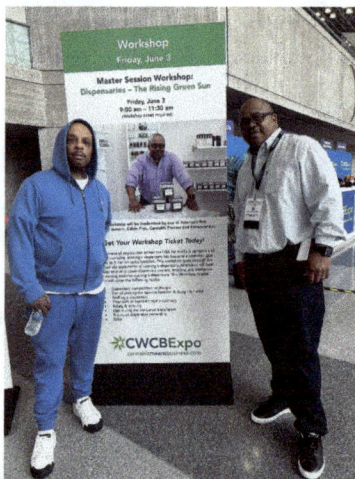

But let's delve deeper. It's not just about having a Rolodex brimming with contacts. It's about cultivating meaningful relationships with those who can mentor you, challenge you, and ultimately open doors. It's about demonstrating your value to them, not just as a business proposition but as a collaborator in the grand vision of legitimizing and revolutionizing the cannabis experience.

Naturally, there are counterarguments. Some say merit and quality alone should dictate success. They argue that an excellent product will inevitably rise to the top, regardless of who you know. While there's a kernel of truth here, it's akin to planting a seed in a garden and expecting it to thrive without sunlight.

The rebuttal to this is clear: in an industry still shedding its stigmatized skin, reputation is everything. Those with a proven track record act as beacons, guiding consumers through the haze to products they can trust. The endorsement of an industry titan doesn't just elevate a product; it confers upon it a seal of approval that resonates with consumers.

Furthermore, alliances can lead to collaborations that result in innovation. When knowledge is shared, when expertise converges, the whole industry takes a step forward. This is the additional supporting evidence that networking is not a mere accessory to success—it's a driver.

In conclusion, while the quality of your product or service is non-negotiable, the relationships you nurture will determine the altitude of your success. The cannabis pioneers who made millions didn't do so in isolation—they reached out, they connected, and they built empires on the foundations of shared vision and mutual respect. In this industry, who you know weaves the very web on which your dreams either take flight or get entangled and perish. So, ask yourself, who are you reaching out to today? Who holds the keys to the kingdom you seek to build? And more importantly, how will you forge the bonds that will lift you from aspiration to achievement? The answer lies not in the wind but in the will to connect, to communicate, and to conquer.

Experience in the Cannabis Business is Key

I can't stress enough how important it is to team up with someone who has actual cannabis business experience. I have witnessed many big corporations, that were headed by people who weren't from the industry and have failed miserably i. e, (most of the Canadian pioneering companies and a few early American companies like MedMen) However, success in this industry isn't just about what you know—it's about having the hands-on experience that can only be learned through active participation and the right partnerships. The essence of mastery in the cannabis business is not found in textbooks, but in the soil of the grow rooms, the pipettes in the labs, the smiles of satisfied customers, and the shrewd calculations of a microbusiness ledger.

Before you lie a map—a guide that reveals the fundamental aspects of experience necessary for thriving in the cannabis industry. Each point, vital in its own right, is a piece of the larger puzzle that, when assembled, creates a complete picture of success.

The crucial experiences that one must seek in a potential partner or acquire personally include:

1. Cultivation Expertise

2. Manufacturing Prowess

3. Retail Dispensary Management

4. Microbusiness Operations a.

The cornerstone of the cannabis industry is its product, and understanding the delicate art of cultivation is paramount. A partner with a green thumb and a deep understanding of cannabis genetics, soil composition, and climate control can ensure a consistent, high-quality product.

Knowledge of cultivation goes beyond planting seeds; it involves selecting the right strains, optimizing growing conditions, and mastering the harvesting process. This experience ensures that the product meets legal standards and exceeds consumer expectations.

Take, for example, the tale of John GreenThumb, whose decades of experience in cannabis horticulture allowed him to develop a proprietary strain that took the market by

storm, exemplifying how expertise can lead to breakthroughs in product quality.

In practice, this experience translates to fewer crop failures, more efficient use of resources, and the ability to innovate with new strains, ultimately leading to higher profit margins and a sterling reputation.

b.

With cultivation as the foundation, manufacturing prowess is the edifice built atop it. This involves the extraction, refinement, and preparation of cannabis products, a complex symphony of science and precision.

Manufacturing in the cannabis industry is an intricate dance of maintaining purity and potency while adhering to strict regulatory standards. Experience here is indispensable as it affects the quality and safety of the end product.

Consider the story of Extract Labs, whose experienced team turned a small operation into a leading producer of CBD oil, recognized for its purity and potency, showcasing the impact of manufacturing expertise.

From edibles to tinctures, the knowledge of proper manufacturing techniques ensures that the final product stands out in a crowded marketplace, securing customer loyalty and establishing brand integrity.

c.

The face of the cannabis industry is the retail dispensary. It's where the product meets the consumer, and where experience in management becomes a lynchpin to success.

Managing a dispensary requires a blend of customer service, compliance with state and local laws, inventory management, and sales strategy. A partner with experience in this aspect brings a customer-centric approach that can turn a simple transaction into a lasting relationship.

Sarah's Sanctuary, a dispensary renowned for its community feel and customer education programs, exemplifies how a well-managed retail space can become a cornerstone of the local cannabis culture.

Effective dispensary management can increase foot traffic, inspire customer loyalty, and ultimately, elevate sales. It's the stage on which the brand performs, and experience ensures that every act is a hit.

d.

Running a micro business in cannabis is about juggling multiple roles and understanding the interplay between cultivation, manufacturing, and retail. It's the culmination of all experiences.

A microbusiness operator must wear many hats, understanding the intricacies of each facet of the industry while maintaining a bird's eye view of the operation as a whole. This experience is about integration and synergy.

Look no further than the story of MicroCanna Co., which thrived by leveraging its

comprehensive grasp of the industry, proving that a holistic approach to the cannabis business is not just beneficial but necessary for long-term success.

Running a micro business requires a strategic mindset that can pivot between the macro and micro aspects of the industry, ensuring that all parts of the business complement each other and work towards a common goal: sustainable profitability.

As we navigate from the roots to the branches of the cannabis business tree, it becomes clear that experience is not just a single leaf but the entire ecosystem. It's the sum of all parts—cultivation, manufacturing, retail, and micro business operations—that creates a thriving, resilient entity capable of weathering the industry's storms and flourishing in its sunshine.

While embarking on the journey to make millions in the cannabis industry, remember that the partner you choose or the experience you gain should be as rich and diverse as the plant itself. It's this depth of knowledge that will guide you through the labyrinth of regulations, market shifts, and consumer trends, leading you to the treasure trove that lies waiting for the well-prepared pioneer.

In the fast-paced and rapidly evolving world of cannabis commerce, knowledge is not just power—it is the cornerstone of entrepreneurial triumph. As one of the pioneering businesses in the United States' cannabis industry, we comprehend the criticality of experience. The path to millions is not a solo journey; it is a collaborative endeavor where the guide you choose can make all the difference. A knowledgeable partner is not a luxury but a necessity, bringing a wealth of experience in navigating the complex political landscape, offering invaluable consulting advice, and crafting a brand that resonates with consumers.

Recognizing the nuances of the ever-changing rules and regulations, understanding the subtleties of branding, and mastering the art of advertising in this unique sector are not just advantages—they are the components of a blueprint for success. Let us unravel this intricate tapestry, thread by thread, revealing the patterns that will lead to prosperity.

The cannabis industry is ensnared in a web of legal intricacies that can ensnare the uninitiated. Navigating this labyrinth requires a partner who is not merely familiar with the current laws but is also prescient about the direction in which they are heading.

Fluency in the language of cannabis legislation is paramount. A seasoned partner brings to the table an understanding of both state and federal laws, which often exist in a state of contradiction. They can foresee shifts in regulatory frameworks and position your business to pivot swiftly, ensuring compliance and avoiding costly legal entanglements.

Take the case of Emerald Enterprises, a business that thrived under the guidance of a former legislator turned cannabis consultant. Their foresight into regulatory changes allowed them to adapt their operations and seize market opportunities as they arose, often before their competitors even caught wind of them.

Having someone who can interpret the fine print of new bills or reforms can be the difference between capitalizing on a new market segment and being left behind. This expertise ensures that every step you take is on solid ground, legally fortified, and strategically sound. In the verdant fields of the cannabis market, branding isn't just about logos and taglines; it is about carving out a niche in a crowded space and establishing a narrative that speaks to your audience.

A partner with branding savvy can help distill your values and vision into a potent brand identity that captures the essence of your business. They understand market trends and consumer psychology, molding your public persona to appeal to your target demographic.

Consider the rise of Cannabliss, whose memorable branding and targeted messaging were the brainchildren of a marketing maestro with deep roots in the cannabis culture. Their iconic imagery and savvy social campaigns catapulted them from obscurity to a household name.

The right partner can guide you through the branding process, from the conceptualization of your company's image to the selection of packaging that speaks volumes without uttering a word. They understand that in the cannabis industry, your brand is not merely a symbol but a story—one that must resonate with authenticity and appeal.

Advertising in the cannabis sector is not for the faint of heart. With traditional avenues often obstructed, creativity and compliance must walk hand in hand.

A partner well-versed in cannabis marketing knows how to circumnavigate the advertising restrictions that stifle less-informed businesses. They push the envelope without tearing it, leveraging unconventional platforms and strategies to reach consumers.

Green Horizons' success story is a testament to the power of innovative advertising. They embraced content marketing and community engagement, building a loyal following that looked beyond the smoke and mirrors of flashy ads to the substance of the brand.

A knowledgeable partner can help you employ guerrilla marketing tactics, harness the power of social media influencers, and engage with communities in meaningful ways that transcend traditional advertising.

As we weave through these critical facets of cannabis business acumen, it becomes clear that the right partnership is not just a boon but a beacon. One that leads through the fog of uncertainty and into the clarity of opportunity. So, ask yourself: does your partner in the cannabis journey possess the insight, the foresight, and the visionary light to illuminate the path to success? The answer will determine not just the potential of your business, but its reality.

Remember, in the cannabis industry, experience doesn't just open doors—it creates them.

Tradeshows and Networking

Imagine stepping into a bustling convention center, the air electric with anticipation and the collective energy of thousands of entrepreneurs, investors, and enthusiasts all converging for a singular purpose: to forge the future of the cannabis industry. This is the scene at a cannabis tradeshow, a nexus of innovation, education, and connection that has become an indispensable arena for anyone serious about making their mark in this burgeoning field.

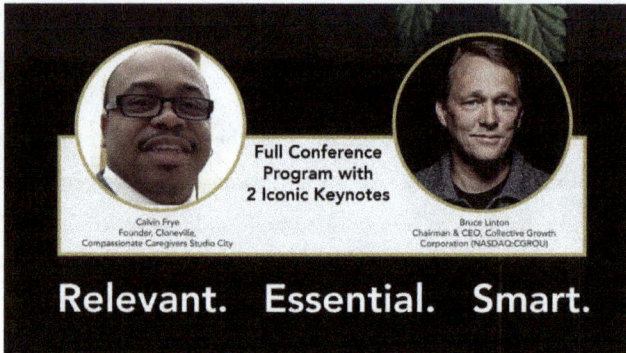

Tradeshows are the beating heart of the cannabis business community, offering a rare opportunity to immerse oneself in the latest trends, products, and ideas shaping the industry. Here, one finds a melting pot of individuals, from seasoned cultivators with their time-tested wisdom to tech-savvy startups disrupting the status quo with cutting-edge solutions. It's at these events that the pulse of the industry can be truly felt and where the seeds of multimillion-dollar deals are often sown.

Networking at these events is not just important; it's the lifeblood of any ambitious cannabis enterprise. It's where relationships are forged, partnerships are nurtured, and alliances are formed. But it's not just about exchanging business cards and making small talk over cocktails. It's about connecting on a deeper level, understanding the unique challenges and aspirations of your peers, and discovering how you can add value to each other's endeavors.

Take, for instance, the story of GreenTech Solutions, a once-small startup that I encountered at a tradeshow a few years back. They were on the brink of a breakthrough with their eco-friendly packaging for cannabis products but struggled to find a distributor who shared their vision for sustainability. At the tradeshow, they networked relentlessly, sharing their passion and the science behind their product with anyone who would listen. It was there that they met a representative from Eco Distributors, a company that was equally passionate about reducing the industry's carbon footprint.

The challenges they faced were clear: breaking through the noise of a crowded marketplace and finding a partner who wasn't just interested in the bottom line but was committed to the ethos of environmental responsibility. Their strategy was equally clear: to leverage the power of storytelling and personal connection, to not just sell a product but to share a mission.

The results were transformative. GreenTech Solutions' partnership with Eco Distributors allowed them to scale up production, reduce costs, and ultimately become a leading name in sustainable cannabis packaging. Their success was a testament to the power of networking, showing that the right conversation with the right person can change everything.

Reflecting on their journey, one can't help but acknowledge the role chance plays in these encounters. But it also underscores the importance of being prepared, of having a compelling narrative, and of being open to collaboration and new ideas. The tradeshows and networking events are the crucibles in which these elements are tested and forged into the gold of opportunity.

As you walk the floor of a tradeshow, you'll see the evidence of success stories in every booth and hear the buzz of potential in every conversation. But the true magic lies in the less tangible realm of human connection, in the shared laughter over a cup of coffee, the empathetic nod when discussing regulatory hurdles, or the spark of excitement when a new concept resonates.

So, why do we network? Why do we travel miles and invest countless hours in these gatherings? Because, in the end, the cannabis industry is not just about plants and profits

—it's about people. It's about the collective striving toward a future where this remarkable plant can achieve its full healing potential, for innovation, and economic prosperity.

As you ponder the power of networking and tradeshows, consider this: who will you meet at your next event? What partnerships await you? And how will these connections propel your business into the echelons of the industry's elite?

Remember, the journey to millions in the cannabis industry is a mosaic of many faces, stories, and handshakes. Each one holds the potential to be the key that unlocks the door to success. The question is, are you ready to turn the handle?
1 2 3 4 5 6 7 8

ABOUT THE AUTHOR

Scientist, pioneering cannabis activist, entrepreneur, and MSO business license holder, Calvin Frye has over 19 years of experience as a dispensary owner and Medical Marijuana (MMJ) industry consultant. He currently has an equity stake in licensees in California, Oklahoma, and Illinois and is currently working with applications on the East Coast market as well. He currently has a partnership with a dispensary chain in Thailand under his Hip Hop Legacy Brand. He is on the advisory board for the Cannabis World Cannabis Business Exposition. Mr. Frye was recently awarded, as part owner, one of the highly sought-after West Hollywood edible consumption lounge licenses. Mr. Frye has held several key positions in the Biotech industry for major companies like Xoma, Amgen, and Baxter Biosciences, advancing his career from Research Associate to Associate Scientist. Mr. Frye has invaluable experience working alongside some of the founders of the MMJ industry (Dennis Peron and Richard Eastman) as well as many of the industry pioneering groups in Los Angeles (Americans for Safe Access and Norml). Mr. Frye also has been appointed to the National Hemp Association's Social Equity Standing Committee and was recently promoted to the chairman of that committee. Mr. Frye has one of the oldest pre-ICO licenses in Los Angeles and is one of the first dispensary owners in the entire country. He has been pivotal in the progression of the cannabis movement throughout the United States. As an activist, Mr. Frye travels all over the United States to help shape and pass current MMJ legislation. He has appeared in numerous documentaries and television shows and has been featured in many magazines as one of the premier voices in cannabis. Nationally, Mr. Frye has been the featured speaker at many conferences including the World Congress Cannabis Expo, Blunt Talks, etc. Mr. Frye has first-hand knowledge of the regulatory issues affecting the cannabis industry through his extensive work with local LA government bodies and agencies. Currently, he is participating in the sponsored mentorship program that oversees and teaches social equity program owners how to operate and run a successful dispensary for the City of Los Angeles. Mr. Frye has also branded his line of cannabis genetics and trademarked the name "Cloneville" which he has attached to his genetics. In 2009, Mr. Frye consulted in the hydroponics industry where he gained extensive knowledge in the actual growing, setup, and production of cannabis. Mr. Frye also owns Frye Consulting and Management Group, a full-service firm that provides consulting services from startup to full-scale production, including regulatory expertise. Mr. Frye earned his Bachelor of Science degree from the University of Iowa (Big Ten Conference) in Science Education. He also attended graduate college with an emphasis in General Science.

Check out a more detailed Bio along with media at realcalvinfrye.com

ACKNOWLEDGEMENTS

First, I would like to acknowledge my family, Toni, Jahkeem, and Leedia, for always giving me the inspiration to keep moving forward. I'd also like to thank my parents Josephine and Willie and all my brothers and sisters, who keep me sharp and focused on becoming successful.

Next, I would like to thank the cannabis industry for allowing me to participate and for being fearful in the eyes of controversy. I would like to thank the ever-evolving technology that helps regular guys like me utilize technology so that we can put our words into books.

Last, but not least, I would like to thank the God within, and the ever-present God within the universe, the creator, for keeping me motivated to do the actual work!

Insider Tips on Making Millions in the Cannabis Industry

1. https://www.nerdwallet.com/article/small-business/how-to-start-a-marijuana-business

   https://www.quicksprout.com/how-to-start-a-cannabis-business/

   https://insights.mjbizdaily.com/factbook-2023/

   https://quantum9.net/virginia-cannabis-license-consulting/

   https://www.findlaw.com/cannabis-law/starting-a-cannabis-business.html

   https://upmetrics.co/start-business/cannabis

   https://www.cannabiz.media/blog/10-factors-that-determine-a-marijuana-entrepreneurs-success-or-failure

   https://cannabiscareer.com/different-cannabis-businesses/

   https://www.leafly.com/news/industry/cannabis-business-models-101

   https://upmetrics.co/template/marijuana-business-plan-example

   https://cannabusinessplans.com/cannabis-business-plan-sample/

   https://www.growthink.com/businessplan/help-center/cannabis-business-plan

   https://www.wolterskluwer.com/en/expert-insights/what-are-business-license-requirements-for-cannabis-businesses

   https://upmetrics.co/start-business/cannabis

   https://www.wolterskluwer.com/en/expert-insights/how-to-obtain-a-retail-marijuana-dispensary-license

   https://cannabis.ca.gov/applicants/license-types/

2. https://www.growthink.com/businessplan/help-center/cannabis-cultivation-business-plan

   https://www.findlaw.com/cannabis-law/starting-a-cannabis-business/marijuana-dispensary-business-plan-example.html

   https://cannabusinessplans.com/cannabis-dispensary-business-plan/

   https://www.sf.gov/information/cannabis-manufacturing-business-operations

   https://cannabis.ca.gov/licensees/manufacturing/

   https://cannabusinessplans.com/cannabis-testing-laboratory-business-plan/

   https://www.treez.io/blog/ultimate-guide-to-write-a-cannabis-business-plan

   https://cannabis.ny.gov/cannabis-laboratories

   https://www.ers.usda.gov/topics/farm-practices-management/risk-management/risk-in-agriculture/

   https://www.investopedia.com/biggest-challenges-for-the-cannabis-industry-in-2019-4583874

   https://www.forbes.com/sites/nickkovacevich/2019/02/01/the-hidden-costs-of-the-cannabis-business/

3. https://indicaonline.com/blog/the-real-cost-of-opening-a-dispensary/

https://www.investopedia.com/terms/a/agribusiness.asp

https://indicaonline.com/blog/the-real-cost-of-opening-a-dispensary/

https://www.smith-howard.com/accounting-challenges-for-cannabis-businesses/

https://polstontax.com/common-accounting-problems-that-cannabis-businesses-face/

https://jcannabisresearch.biomedcentral.com/articles/10.1186/s42238-020-00049-7

https://www.politico.com/news/2022/09/04/weed-companies-cant-make-money-00054541

https://greengrowthcpas.com/top-5-reasons-cannabis-businesses-fail-and-how-to-avoid-them/

https://www.bloomberglaw.com/external/document/XFAEEE8000000/finance-professional-perspective-debt-financing-in-the-cannabis-

https://greengrowthcpas.com/best-practices-for-managing-cash-flow/

https://www.covasoftware.com/blog/best-practices-in-cash-management-for-cannabis-

https://www.harrisbeach.com/insights/capital-financing-options-for-new-yorks-burgeoning-cannabis-industry/

https://www.redbudadvisors.com/post/starting-a-cannabis-business-a-guide-to-overcoming-challenges-and-ensuring-success

4. https://www.redbudadvisors.com/post/starting-a-cannabis-business-a-guide-to-overcoming-challenges-and-ensuring-success
https://www.flourishsoftware.com/blog/cannabis-accounting-best-practices
https://cannabistech.com/contributed/financial-strategies-in-cannabis/
https://greengrowthcpas.com/best-practices-for-managing-cash-flow/
https://polstontax.com/marijuana-banking-101-how-to-manage-your-money-in-the-cannabis-business/
https://polstontax.com/ways-to-boost-financial-success-of-your-cannabis-business/
https://cannabis.ca.gov/licensees/cultivation/
https://dec.vermont.gov/air-quality/permits/source-categories/cannabis-cultivation-and-processing
https://cannabis.ny.gov/system/files/documents/2023/12/ocm-aucultivation.pdf
https://www.lawinsider.com/dictionary/cannabis-cultivation
https://www.paradise-seeds.com/grow-weed/awesome-cannabis-grow-techniques/
https://sumocannabis.com/en/the-different-methods-of-cultivating-cannabis/

5. https://cannabis.ca.gov/licensees/manufacturing/

https://www.cdph.ca.gov/Programs/CEH/DFD-CS/MCSB/CDPH%20Document%20Library/LicenseTypes.pdf

https://www.fda.gov/news-events/public-health-focus/fda-regulation-cannabis-and-cannabis-derived-products-including-cannabidiol-cbd

https://www.420property.com/listings/equipment/

https://www.visualcapitalist.com/sp/every-cannabis-product-in-one-graphic/

https://www.medicalnewstoday.com/articles/types-of-cbd

https://www.nyc.gov/assets/buildings/pdf/canbiz-rd.pdf

https://www.kayapush.com/blog/how-to-open-a-dispensary-creating-a-business-plan

https://www.nj.gov/cannabis/businesses/

https://www.covasoftware.com/how-to-open-a-dispensary

https://cannabis.ny.gov/system/files/documents/2023/12/ocm-aumicrobusiness.pdf

https://koronapos.com/blog/marijuana-microbusinesses/

https://polstontax.com/how-to-structure-your-marijuana-business-incorporation-vs-llc/

https://vangst.com/blog/vertical-integration-cannabis

https://www.andretaxco.com/non-plant-touching-cannabis-credit

https://www.joyflo.co/blog/ancillary-cannabis-businesses-beyond-the-plant-touching-boundaries

6. https://www.businessnewsdaily.com/15812-cannabis-industry-business-growth.html

   https://www.covasoftware.com/blog/how-to-write-a-cannabis-business-plan

   https://www.wolterskluwer.com/en/expert-insights/what-are-business-license-requirements-for-cannabis-businesses

   https://www.covasoftware.com/how-to-open-a-dispensary

   https://www.wolterskluwer.com/en/expert-insights/how-to-obtain-a-retail-marijuana-dispensary-license

   https://www.covasoftware.com/how-to-open-a-dispensary

   https://cannabis.ca.gov/applicants/how-to-apply/

   https://cannabis.ny.gov/system/files/documents/2023/12/ocm-augeneral.pdf

   https://cannabis.ca.gov/applicants/how-to-apply/

   https://www.findlaw.com/cannabis-law/starting-a-cannabis-business/how-to-get-financing-for-a-marijuana-business.html

   https://cannabizteam.com/2022/02/how-to-get-funding-for-your-cannabis-business/

   https://www.order.co/blog/finance/cannabis-financing/

   https://www.flourishsoftware.com/blog/how-to-fund-your-cannabis-business

   https://www.cannabisindustrylawyer.com/how-to-raise-funds-for-your-cannabis-company/

7. https://qredible.com/cannabis-branding-strategies-a-helpful-guide/

   https://www.enthuse-marketing.com/pillars-for-a-winning-cannabis-marketing-strategy/

   https://www.hoodcollective.com/post/why-your-brand-is-your-cannabis-company-s-most-important-asset

   https://www.mygrasslands.com/cannabis-marketing/why-is-marketing-cannabis-so-important

   https://www.enthuse-marketing.com/pillars-for-a-winning-cannabis-marketing-strategy/

   https://www.exponents.com/our-blog/top-cannabis-trade-shows-in-usa/

   https://cannabispromotions.com/how-to-market-your-cannabis-brand-through-events/

   https://cannabispromotions.com/how-to-be-successful-at-a-cannabis-trade-show/

   https://www.cannabiz.media/blog/virtual-cannabis-industry-conferences-how-to-promote-your-business-with-email-marketing

   https://paybotic.com/learn/blog/decoding-the-art-of-cannabis-marketing-top-10-strategies

8. https://www.forbes.com/sites/roberthoban/2020/08/31/the-critical-importance-of-social-equity-in-the-cannabis-industry/

https://flowhub.com/cannabis-social-equity-programs-complete-guide

https://norml.org/laws/expungement/

https://leafwell.com/blog/8-black-owned-cannabis-dispensaries-to-visit-around-the-u-s

https://flowhub.com/social-equity-program

https://fortune.com/2022/04/26/black-cannabis-entrepreneurs-marijuana-businesses-marijuana-laws/

https://cannabis.ny.gov/system/files/documents/2023/09/nys-see-plan-english.pdf

https://dceo.illinois.gov/cannabisequity/socialequityapplicantcriteria.html

https://minoritycannabis.org/equitymap/illinois/equity-illinois/

https://mjbizdaily.com/progress-not-happening-fast-enough-for-cannabis-social-equity-entrepreneurs/

https://www.forbes.com/sites/kriskrane/2023/08/01/whats-killing-social-equity-in-cannabis-lack-of-banking/

https://www.reuters.com/legal/litigation/challenges-getting-social-equity-right-state-legal-cannabis-industry-2021-07-22/

https://www.americanbar.org/groups/tort_trial_insurance_practice/publications/tortsource/2022/spring/social-equity-cannabis/

https://www.linkedin.com/pulse/social-equity-challenges-cannabis-industry-remy-arteaga

www.ingramcontent.com/pod-product-compliance
Lightning Source LLC
Chambersburg PA
CBHW071705210326
41597CB00017B/2348